Data Science in Action: From Data Wrangling to Predictive Modeling

James Relington

DEDICATION

To those who seek knowledge, inspiration, and new perspectives—
may this book be a companion on your journey, a spark for curiosity,
and a reminder that every page turned is a step toward discovery.

AKNOWLEDGEMENTS

I would like to express my deepest gratitude to everyone who contributed to the creation of this book. To my colleagues and mentors, your insights and expertise have been invaluable. A special thank you to my family and friends for their unwavering support and encouragement throughout this journey.

Foundations of Data Science

Data science stands at the intersection of multiple disciplines, blending elements of computer science, mathematics, statistics, and domain expertise to extract knowledge and actionable insights from data. Its foundations are deeply rooted in the scientific method, requiring practitioners to pose hypotheses, gather relevant data, perform analysis, and evaluate findings to guide decision-making. In today's increasingly digitized world, data science serves as the backbone of innovation across industries, enabling organizations to understand patterns, predict outcomes, and automate processes in ways that were once unimaginable. As a field, it represents both a methodological approach to understanding the world and a technological framework for solving real-world problems with data-driven strategies.

At its core, data science is about asking the right questions. Before any model is trained or data visualized, a clear understanding of the problem is necessary. This begins with framing a business or research challenge into a data question. A well-posed question is essential because it determines the type of data required, the tools needed, and the form of analysis that will yield the most meaningful results. Data scientists must work closely with stakeholders to clarify objectives, uncover hidden assumptions, and translate vague goals into precise analytical tasks. This preliminary step often distinguishes successful data science projects from those that fail to deliver value.

Once the problem is clearly defined, the next phase involves data acquisition and exploration. Data can come from a wide range of sources, including databases, APIs, sensors, social media platforms, transaction logs, or surveys. The raw data collected is rarely ready for immediate analysis. It is frequently messy, incomplete, inconsistent, or unstructured. Therefore, one of the foundational tasks in data science is data wrangling—cleaning, transforming, and structuring the data so that it can be analyzed efficiently and effectively. This is where domain knowledge becomes invaluable. Understanding the context in which the data was generated helps identify errors, anomalies, and outliers that might otherwise go unnoticed.

With clean data in hand, the next logical step is exploratory data analysis (EDA), a process that involves summarizing the main characteristics of the data, often using visualizations. EDA allows data scientists to discover patterns, spot trends, and test initial hypotheses. It plays a critical role in guiding subsequent modeling efforts by revealing correlations, distributions, and relationships within the dataset. Through EDA, practitioners gain a deeper understanding of the variables at play and can begin to make informed decisions about which features to include, how to handle missing values, and what transformations might improve the predictive power of models.

Modeling is often the most visible aspect of data science, but it is only one part of a broader process. Selecting the right algorithm depends on the nature of the problem, the structure of the data, and the intended outcome. For instance, classification models are used to assign labels to categories, while regression models predict continuous values. Clustering techniques uncover natural groupings within data, and dimensionality reduction methods simplify complex datasets without sacrificing essential information. The performance of these models is evaluated using statistical metrics, which help determine their accuracy, precision, recall, and overall effectiveness. However, a model's utility extends beyond numbers; it must also be interpretable, fair, and aligned with the goals of the project.

Technology plays a crucial role in data science. Languages like Python and R have become industry standards due to their rich ecosystems of libraries and frameworks tailored for data manipulation, statistical analysis, and machine learning. Tools like Jupyter Notebooks provide interactive environments for experimentation, while version control systems like Git ensure reproducibility and collaboration. Databases such as SQL-based systems or NoSQL solutions offer ways to store and retrieve data efficiently. Meanwhile, cloud computing platforms provide the scalability necessary to handle large datasets and perform computations at scale. A strong grasp of these technologies is essential for any aspiring data scientist.

Equally important is the ability to communicate findings effectively. Data science is not only about building models but also about telling compelling stories with data. Visualization tools such as Matplotlib, Seaborn, and Tableau help convey complex insights in an accessible way. Reports and presentations must be tailored to their audience, whether they are technical colleagues, business executives, or the general public. The goal is not just to present results, but to enable informed decision-making by highlighting the implications of those results. A successful data scientist must therefore be a skilled communicator, capable of bridging the gap between data and action.

Ethics also forms a foundational pillar of data science. As models increasingly influence decisions in hiring, healthcare, finance, and law enforcement, concerns about bias, fairness, and transparency have come to the forefront. Data scientists must be vigilant about the potential societal impact of their work, ensuring that data is used responsibly and that algorithms do not perpetuate or amplify existing inequalities. This requires a commitment to rigorous testing, transparency in methodology, and ongoing evaluation of outcomes. Understanding the ethical dimensions of data science is essential to building systems that are not only effective but also just and trustworthy.

The field of data science is inherently interdisciplinary, requiring collaboration across roles and expertise. Data engineers ensure that infrastructure is in place to handle data flows, while statisticians contribute rigorous methods for inference. Machine learning engineers help productionize models, and domain experts provide the contextual knowledge that grounds analysis in reality. Success in data science depends not only on technical prowess but also on the ability to work across teams, understand different perspectives, and integrate diverse forms of knowledge into coherent solutions.

As data becomes increasingly central to all aspects of life and business, the importance of a strong foundation in data science continues to grow. Whether predicting customer behavior, optimizing logistics, diagnosing diseases, or combating climate change, data science offers the tools to tackle complex challenges with precision and creativity. But to harness its full potential, practitioners must ground themselves in the principles that underlie the field: critical thinking, rigorous analysis, technological fluency, ethical awareness, and a relentless curiosity about the world. Only by building on these foundations can data science truly fulfill its promise as a transformative force in the modern age.

Understanding the Data Science Lifecycle

Understanding the data science lifecycle is essential for any practitioner aiming to create value from data. This lifecycle is not a rigid sequence of tasks, but rather a dynamic, iterative process that guides the development of data-driven solutions from conception to deployment and monitoring. It provides a structured framework for navigating the complexity of data science projects, ensuring that each stage builds logically upon the previous one and contributes meaningfully to the final objective. By appreciating the flow and interdependence of each phase, data scientists can approach challenges with greater clarity and effectiveness, adapting as necessary to the evolving nature of data, business needs, and technological constraints.

The lifecycle typically begins with problem definition. At this initial stage, collaboration between data scientists and stakeholders is critical. The goal is to clearly articulate the business or research question that the project seeks to answer. This involves understanding the broader context in which the problem exists, identifying the key metrics or outcomes of interest, and determining whether a data-driven approach is appropriate. This phase requires careful questioning and an ability to translate vague or complex requirements into specific, measurable objectives that can guide the entire project. Without a well-defined problem, even the most sophisticated models may fail to deliver useful or actionable insights.

Following problem definition, the focus shifts to data acquisition. This involves identifying the sources of data that are relevant to the problem and obtaining access to them in a secure and compliant manner. Data can come from internal systems, such as customer databases or operational logs, or from external sources, including open datasets, APIs, third-party providers, or IoT devices. The diversity of data types—structured, unstructured, time-series, geospatial, or text—adds complexity to this phase. A thorough understanding of the data sources and the mechanisms of data collection is crucial for ensuring that the subsequent analysis is based on accurate, relevant, and timely information.

Once the data has been acquired, the next phase is data preparation. This step, often referred to as data wrangling or data cleaning, is one of the most time-consuming aspects of the data science lifecycle. Raw data is rarely analysis-ready. It may contain missing values, duplicate entries, inconsistent formatting, or noisy and irrelevant information. The process of preparing data involves identifying and correcting these issues, standardizing formats, transforming variables, handling outliers, and engineering new features that may enhance model performance. This step requires a balance of technical skill and domain knowledge, as well as an awareness of how data quality affects the reliability of insights and models.

With a clean and structured dataset in place, the next phase is exploratory data analysis. This is where data scientists begin to extract initial insights and form hypotheses about the underlying patterns in the data. Visualizations, statistical summaries, and correlation analyses are common tools used during this stage. The objective is to better understand the distribution of variables, the relationships between features, and the potential predictors of the target outcome. Exploratory data analysis also plays a critical role in uncovering biases, anomalies, or data limitations that may influence the interpretation of results or the design of machine learning models.

The modeling phase is the centerpiece of the data science lifecycle. In this stage, data scientists select appropriate algorithms to build predictive or descriptive models based on the prepared data. The choice of model depends on the nature of the problem—classification, regression, clustering, or recommendation—as well as the characteristics of the dataset. Training and testing are performed using various validation techniques to assess model performance and generalizability. Metrics such as accuracy, precision, recall, F1 score, ROC-AUC, and others are used to evaluate how well the model meets the defined objectives. This phase often requires multiple iterations of tuning and optimization, including hyperparameter adjustment and feature selection, to achieve the desired results.

After a model has been trained and validated, the deployment phase comes into focus. Deployment involves integrating the model into a production environment where it can be accessed by users or systems to make real-time or batch predictions. This step may involve developing APIs, building dashboards, or embedding the model into an existing application. The deployment process also includes considerations for scalability, performance, and security. Model monitoring is essential to ensure that the system behaves as expected over time, particularly as new data enters the ecosystem and as user behavior or external conditions change. A model that performs well in development may degrade in production if not carefully monitored and maintained.

The final, but ongoing, phase of the data science lifecycle is feedback and iteration. Data science is not a one-and-done endeavor. Once deployed, models and insights must be continuously evaluated in the real world to ensure they remain accurate and relevant. Feedback from users, business metrics, and updated datasets provide the basis for refining models, retraining with new data, and adjusting strategies. This iterative loop is what makes data science both powerful and challenging—it is a living process that adapts to change, learns from outcomes, and evolves with the needs of the organization or the research question at hand.

Throughout the lifecycle, communication plays a pivotal role. Data scientists must document their processes, articulate assumptions, justify decisions, and present results in ways that are understandable to both technical and non-technical stakeholders. Clear and transparent communication ensures that insights are trusted and that decisions based on data are made with full awareness of the model's strengths and limitations. This transparency is also essential for ethical accountability, especially in high-stakes domains where data-driven decisions can significantly impact individuals and communities.

The data science lifecycle is not a linear pathway, but rather a cyclical, feedback-rich journey through problem-solving. Each phase builds on the previous one, but also informs and revises earlier steps as new insights emerge. Mastering this lifecycle requires not only technical proficiency and analytical thinking but also adaptability, curiosity, and a collaborative mindset. It is through this comprehensive, iterative process that data scientists can transform raw information into meaningful action, turning complex challenges into opportunities for innovation and discovery.

Exploring Types of Data

Understanding the various types of data is fundamental to mastering data science. The type of data influences every subsequent decision in a project, from the selection of algorithms to the preprocessing steps and visualization methods. Data can manifest in multiple forms, and each type brings its own characteristics, benefits, and challenges. For a data scientist, being able to distinguish between these types and knowing how to handle them effectively is as essential as knowing how to write code or build models. Data types are not just labels; they represent how information is structured and interpreted, ultimately determining the techniques suitable for analysis and the insights that can be extracted.

At the highest level, data can be broadly categorized as structured or unstructured. Structured data refers to information that is organized in a tabular format, often stored in relational databases. This kind of data includes rows and columns where each column represents a specific variable and each row corresponds to a single record. Structured data is highly organized and easy to query using SQL or data frames in programming languages like Python or R. Examples include customer purchase records, sales transactions, sensor readings, and survey results. This data is typically numeric or categorical, and because of its consistent format, it is well-suited for statistical analysis and machine learning.

Unstructured data, on the other hand, lacks a predefined format. It is more complex and diverse, encompassing a wide variety of content types such as text, images, audio, and video. Emails, social media posts, legal documents, news articles, medical imaging, and surveillance footage all fall into this category. Since unstructured data does not fit neatly into rows and columns, it often requires advanced processing techniques like natural language processing for text or computer vision for images. Despite its complexity, unstructured data contains rich contextual information and is growing rapidly in importance as organizations seek to analyze sentiment, behavior, and other abstract qualities not captured by traditional structured formats.

Within structured data, a further breakdown reveals numerical and categorical data. Numerical data consists of values that represent measurable quantities. These can be either discrete or continuous. Discrete numerical data consists of whole numbers that typically count occurrences or items, such as the number of children in a household or the number of clicks on a webpage. Continuous numerical data includes any values within a range and can be infinitely divisible, like temperature readings, weight, or time. These values are essential for quantitative analysis, enabling computations such as means, variances, and correlations that form the backbone of statistical modeling.

Categorical data, by contrast, refers to variables that represent categories or groups rather than measurable quantities. This data type includes nominal and ordinal categories. Nominal data has no inherent order; examples include colors, types of cuisine, or names of cities. Each value represents a distinct class with no logical sequencing. Ordinal data, however, includes categories with a meaningful order, such as rating scales, education levels, or product sizes. While ordinal values can be ranked, the intervals between them are not necessarily equal or interpretable. Properly identifying categorical variables is vital, especially because machine learning algorithms often require special treatment such as encoding these values into a numerical format before they can be processed.

Another critical data type is time series data, which involves observations recorded at successive points in time. This kind of data is particularly prevalent in fields such as finance, meteorology, and industrial monitoring. Time series data is unique in that it has a temporal component, meaning the order of the data matters and the observations are often correlated with one another over time. Analyzing time series data requires techniques that account for trends, seasonality, and autocorrelation, making it distinct from other types of data. Tools like rolling averages, exponential smoothing, and ARIMA models are commonly employed to uncover patterns and forecast future values.

Text data is an increasingly important type of unstructured data. It includes everything from product reviews and support tickets to research articles and social media conversations. Unlike numerical data, text is composed of words and sentences, which must be parsed and analyzed using specialized techniques. Natural language processing allows data scientists to extract meaning from text through tokenization, sentiment analysis, named entity recognition, and other linguistic transformations. The richness of text data offers insights into opinion, intent, and context, making it a valuable resource for understanding human communication at scale.

Image and audio data also play a significant role in data science, especially in areas involving deep learning. Image data consists of pixels arranged in grids, where each pixel represents color or intensity values. Processing image data requires understanding both the spatial structure and the content of the image. Techniques such as convolutional neural networks have revolutionized image recognition and classification tasks. Similarly, audio data, which involves waveforms or spectrograms, is essential in applications like voice recognition, music classification, and sound event detection. Working with these data types often requires domain-specific knowledge, advanced computing resources, and access to large annotated datasets for training models effectively.

A newer and increasingly relevant category is geospatial data. This type of data includes information tied to geographical locations, such as GPS coordinates, addresses, or map overlays. Geospatial data is used in urban planning, logistics, environmental monitoring, and public health. Its analysis requires understanding of spatial relationships and techniques such as geocoding, spatial joins, and distance calculations. Tools like Geographic Information Systems (GIS) and libraries such as GeoPandas enable the manipulation and visualization of location-based data, opening new possibilities for analysis in both commercial and scientific domains.

Data can also be classified based on its level of measurement. These include nominal, ordinal, interval, and ratio scales. Each level provides different opportunities and limitations for analysis. For instance, interval data has meaningful differences between values but lacks a true zero point, like temperature in Celsius. Ratio data, like weight or height, includes both equal intervals and an absolute zero, allowing for the full range of mathematical operations. Understanding the measurement level of a dataset ensures the correct application of statistical tests and analytical techniques, thus safeguarding the validity of the results.

A nuanced understanding of data types allows data scientists to tailor their approaches, avoid methodological errors, and maximize the insights gained from analysis. It influences how missing data is handled, how variables are transformed, how models interpret inputs, and how results are communicated to stakeholders. The diversity of data types also reflects the diversity of human knowledge and experience, challenging data scientists to adapt their skills to an ever-expanding universe of information. Mastering these types is not merely about classification; it is about understanding the underlying structure of information and the most effective way to extract meaning from it.

Data Collection Techniques and Tools

Data collection is the cornerstone of any data science project, setting the foundation for all subsequent analysis, modeling, and interpretation. Without reliable and relevant data, even the most advanced algorithms cannot produce meaningful insights. Data collection refers to the process of gathering information from various sources in a way that ensures its quality, accuracy, and appropriateness for solving a particular problem. The effectiveness of a data science workflow begins with the techniques and tools used to acquire the data. As such, understanding how to collect data efficiently and ethically is one of the most critical skills a data scientist can develop.

There are numerous methods for collecting data, each suitable for different types of projects and objectives. One of the most common approaches is direct data entry through manual input. This includes surveys, forms, and interviews where individuals provide information that is later aggregated and analyzed. Although manual entry is time-consuming and potentially prone to human error, it is invaluable when collecting subjective or personalized data, such as opinions, preferences, or behavioral feedback. Designing forms and questionnaires that yield clear, unbiased responses is an art in itself, requiring attention to question structure, response format, and user experience.

Another major technique involves the automated collection of data from digital sources. In today's connected world, websites, mobile applications, and IoT devices generate vast amounts of data continuously. Web scraping is a powerful method to extract data from websites, using tools and libraries that simulate browser behavior and parse HTML content. Python libraries like BeautifulSoup and Scrapy are widely used for this purpose, allowing data scientists to programmatically collect information from online directories, product pages, news articles, or social media posts. However, scraping must be conducted responsibly, with awareness of website terms of service, ethical considerations, and legal restrictions.

In addition to scraping, application programming interfaces, or APIs, provide structured access to data from online platforms and services. APIs are standardized ways for programs to communicate with one another, and many organizations offer public or private APIs to share datasets. For example, social media platforms like Twitter and Reddit provide APIs to access user posts and engagement metrics. Financial data, weather information, sports statistics, and government records are also commonly available through APIs. APIs are often preferred over scraping because they provide data in a clean, structured format such as JSON or XML, reducing the need for heavy preprocessing and enhancing the reliability of the data.

Sensor-based data collection represents another rapidly growing domain, especially in industries such as manufacturing, agriculture, and healthcare. Sensors embedded in machinery, vehicles, or wearable devices continuously generate data points that reflect physical conditions such as temperature, humidity, motion, or pressure. The Internet of Things enables the remote collection and transmission of this data, feeding it into centralized systems for analysis and decision-making. This kind of real-time, high-frequency data poses unique challenges related to volume, velocity, and variety, but it also provides unparalleled opportunities for predictive maintenance, real-time monitoring, and automation.

Transactional data is another rich source of information. Every digital interaction, from online purchases and banking activities to supply chain events and customer service logs, generates a record that can be collected and analyzed. Most of this data is stored in relational databases, which can be accessed using SQL. Data scientists must be proficient in querying these systems to extract relevant subsets of information. Structured Query Language remains a foundational tool for interacting with large-scale data storage systems, enabling filtering, joining, and aggregating data in powerful ways. Beyond traditional databases, modern data lakes and warehouses offer scalable solutions for storing and querying massive datasets from multiple sources in diverse formats.

Mobile applications and embedded software systems also offer unique pathways for data collection. App developers often include analytics tools that track user behavior within an application, capturing metrics such as click paths, session duration, and feature usage. Tools like Google Analytics, Mixpanel, and Firebase provide dashboards and APIs to access this user interaction data, which is essential for improving user experience, targeting content, and driving business strategy. This behavioral data must be collected with transparency and respect for privacy regulations, ensuring that users are aware of what is being tracked and how their information is used.

Crowdsourcing has emerged as a novel method of data collection, leveraging the power of distributed human contributors to gather or validate data. Platforms like Amazon Mechanical Turk allow organizations to outsource data labeling, transcription, image recognition, and survey participation to a global workforce. This approach is especially useful for tasks that require human judgment or contextual understanding. However, crowdsourced data collection demands careful quality control and validation procedures to ensure accuracy and consistency. Incentive structures, task design, and redundancy mechanisms all play a role in maintaining the integrity of the data collected from large groups of contributors.

Social media platforms represent a hybrid space where both structured and unstructured data can be harvested. User-generated content such as tweets, posts, and comments offers a window into public opinion, emerging trends, and collective behavior. Natural language processing techniques can extract meaning from this content, but the collection of social media data requires sensitivity to ethical issues, particularly around user consent and anonymity. The real-time and public nature of social media makes it a valuable source for timely insights, though its noise and variability present technical challenges.

Another important aspect of data collection involves logging systems and telemetry. Software applications and digital platforms often include logging frameworks that capture detailed records of system events, user interactions, and error messages. These logs are a crucial source of information for diagnosing issues, understanding user behavior, and monitoring system performance. Logs can be ingested into centralized platforms like Elasticsearch or Splunk, where they can be searched, filtered, and visualized. The volume of log data can be overwhelming, but when harnessed properly, it offers deep visibility into the inner workings of complex systems.

Data collection does not happen in isolation. It must be guided by clear objectives, an understanding of the problem space, and a commitment to data governance. Ensuring that data is collected in a way that respects user privacy, complies with legal frameworks such as GDPR or HIPAA, and aligns with ethical standards is paramount. Data provenance, or the ability to trace where data came from and how it has been processed, is also critical for ensuring transparency and reproducibility. Modern tools increasingly integrate features that support data governance, metadata tracking, and access control, helping organizations maintain trust and accountability in their data practices.

In the modern data landscape, the tools and techniques available for data collection are constantly evolving. From low-code platforms that simplify the integration of multiple data sources to advanced real-time streaming systems that handle millions of events per second, the ecosystem is both rich and dynamic. A successful data scientist must not only know which tools to use, but also how to combine them creatively to construct robust, flexible, and efficient data pipelines. At its heart, data collection is about building a bridge between raw information and analytical insight, making it one of the most vital stages in the entire data science journey.

APIs and Web Scraping for Data Acquisition

In the world of data science, acquiring reliable and relevant data is a critical first step. Among the various methods for gathering data, two of the most powerful and commonly used techniques are accessing Application Programming Interfaces (APIs) and employing web scraping. These methods allow data scientists to extract valuable information from the web and other digital platforms, enabling them to fuel analysis, build models, and generate insights that would be impossible without access to external data sources. As data becomes increasingly decentralized and dynamic, mastering APIs and web scraping is essential for any data professional aiming to work with real-world, up-to-date datasets.

APIs offer a structured and standardized way to access data that resides on external servers. They act as intermediaries between systems, allowing applications to request and retrieve data in a controlled, efficient manner. APIs are particularly valuable because they return data in machine-readable formats, most commonly JSON or XML, making it straightforward to integrate with analytical tools and workflows. Many organizations expose APIs to share their data with the public or with partners, including governments, social media platforms, financial institutions, and weather services. By using APIs, data scientists can access vast repositories of information, from real-time stock prices and public health statistics to transportation schedules and historical weather records.

The process of using an API typically begins with obtaining the necessary credentials, such as an API key or token. These credentials help providers manage access, monitor usage, and enforce rate limits.

After authentication, data scientists make HTTP requests to specific endpoints, which represent various services or data objects. For instance, an endpoint might return recent tweets from a user, the latest news articles about a topic, or the current temperature in a given location. These requests can include parameters to filter results, specify formats, or paginate through large datasets. The responses, often nested and hierarchical in structure, require parsing and transformation before they are ready for analysis.

Tools like the Python requests library make it easy to interact with APIs. Once the response is received, it can be decoded into a data frame using tools like Pandas, making it ready for exploratory analysis, visualization, or feeding into a machine learning pipeline. Beyond simple GET requests, APIs may also support POST, PUT, and DELETE methods, which are used to submit data, update existing records, or remove entries. However, in data science, GET requests are by far the most commonly used, since the primary goal is usually to acquire rather than modify data.

While APIs provide a clean and efficient way to obtain data, not all sources offer an accessible or open API. In these cases, web scraping becomes a valuable alternative. Web scraping is the practice of extracting information directly from the HTML content of web pages. It involves downloading the web page, parsing the HTML structure, and identifying the elements that contain the desired data. Unlike APIs, web scraping does not depend on formal access channels and can be used to gather data from virtually any public web page, provided it is done in accordance with legal and ethical guidelines.

Web scraping begins with sending a request to the URL of the target web page. The response includes the raw HTML content, which is then parsed using libraries such as BeautifulSoup or lxml in Python. These tools enable the data scientist to navigate the HTML tree, locate specific tags, extract attributes or text, and organize the data into usable formats like lists, dictionaries, or tables. Web scraping can be highly flexible and customized, allowing the user to handle complex layouts, follow pagination, and extract data across multiple pages using loops and dynamic queries.

One of the challenges of web scraping is dealing with inconsistent or frequently changing web structures. Websites may redesign their layouts, change tag names, or load content dynamically using JavaScript. In such cases, static scraping may fail, and more advanced tools like Selenium or Playwright are required. These tools simulate user interaction in a browser environment, allowing data scientists to load dynamic content, click through menus, fill out forms, and scroll through pages to reveal hidden data. While powerful, these approaches are also more resource-intensive and require greater attention to error handling and execution timing.

Respecting the terms of service and legal boundaries is crucial when performing web scraping. Many websites specify in their robots.txt file which areas of their site are off-limits to automated access. Ignoring these restrictions can lead to IP bans or even legal consequences. Ethical scraping practices include respecting rate limits, avoiding excessive server requests, and clearly identifying the scraper with a user-agent string. Where possible, it is always better to use an official API rather than resorting to scraping, as APIs provide a more stable, sanctioned, and respectful means of accessing data.

Both APIs and web scraping serve complementary roles in the data acquisition process. APIs are ideal for structured, reliable, and well-documented data retrieval. They are faster to integrate, less likely to break, and typically offer robust filtering and pagination options. On the other hand, web scraping is indispensable when APIs are unavailable or too limited in scope. It opens the door to unstructured and unique data sources, such as user reviews, product listings, blogs, and real estate advertisements. Data scientists often use both techniques in tandem to build comprehensive datasets that combine the richness of scraped content with the consistency of API-provided data.

The ability to gather data independently gives data scientists autonomy and flexibility in their work. Rather than being limited to predefined datasets or internal databases, they can explore a wide universe of external information to enhance their analyses. Whether predicting customer trends, monitoring competitor behavior, or building recommendation systems, access to timely and relevant data is key. Mastering APIs and web scraping expands the toolbox of a data scientist, allowing for greater creativity, deeper exploration, and a more nuanced understanding of the world through data.

In practical terms, integrating APIs and web scraping into automated workflows is essential for scalability. Cron jobs, cloud functions, and pipeline orchestration tools such as Apache Airflow can schedule and manage regular data collection tasks. Storing the collected data efficiently, managing updates, and ensuring data integrity are equally important. As the ecosystem of online information continues to grow, so does the importance of robust, ethical, and well-designed data acquisition methods. APIs and web scraping are not just technical tools—they are gateways to knowledge, powering the insights and innovations that define modern data science.

Introduction to Data Wrangling

Data wrangling, also known as data munging, is the process of transforming raw data into a format that is clean, consistent, and ready for analysis. In any data science project, the initial dataset is rarely perfect. It often contains missing values, duplicate entries, inconsistencies in formatting, and a variety of other issues that can obstruct meaningful analysis. The process of wrangling this data is not just a preliminary chore—it is a foundational step that determines the quality and reliability of the entire project. Data wrangling is where a data scientist begins to engage deeply with the dataset, uncovering its structure, content, and limitations while preparing it for the more glamorous stages of modeling and interpretation.

The importance of data wrangling cannot be overstated. It is frequently cited that data scientists spend the majority of their time, sometimes up to eighty percent, on cleaning and preparing data. This investment is crucial because no model, no matter how advanced, can overcome the effects of poor-quality input data. Errors, inconsistencies, and irrelevant information can lead to misleading insights or even catastrophic decisions if not addressed early in the pipeline. Data wrangling ensures that the data feeding into statistical models and machine learning algorithms is accurate, complete, and representative of the problem being solved.

At the heart of data wrangling is understanding the nature and structure of the data. This involves examining the types of variables present, identifying relationships between columns, and detecting anomalies. Numerical, categorical, textual, and datetime fields all require different handling strategies. For instance, numerical fields may need normalization, while categorical fields might need encoding or grouping. Date and time information often requires parsing and formatting, especially when dealing with multiple time zones or inconsistent timestamp formats. Gaining familiarity with the data allows the data scientist to make informed decisions about what to keep, modify, or discard.

Handling missing data is one of the central tasks in data wrangling. Real-world datasets often contain null or missing values due to system errors, user input omissions, or simply the nature of the data collection process. The way missing values are treated depends on the context. They can be removed entirely, imputed with statistical measures such as mean or median, or filled using domain-specific knowledge. In some cases, the absence of data itself is informative and may be converted into a feature for modeling. Whatever the approach, consistency and transparency in handling missing data are essential to preserve the integrity of the analysis.

Another frequent issue in raw datasets is the presence of duplicate records. Duplicate data can skew analysis and lead to overrepresented patterns that do not reflect the true distribution. Identifying duplicates involves comparing records based on key fields and determining whether they are exact copies or slight variations. In certain contexts, even slight differences in formatting or spelling might result in duplicate-like records that require deduplication with more sophisticated logic. Removing duplicates is a necessary step to ensure that statistical summaries and model training reflect the true diversity of the dataset.

Standardizing data formats is another key aspect of wrangling. This includes ensuring consistency in how dates, numbers, text, and other types are represented. For instance, numerical values should be represented using the same units and precision, dates should follow a uniform format, and text fields should be normalized to remove irregular capitalization, extra spaces, or special characters. These transformations make it easier to manipulate and analyze the data programmatically, reducing the risk of errors during later stages of the project. Consistent formatting also facilitates merging and joining datasets, which is common when combining data from multiple sources.

Data wrangling also involves detecting and correcting outliers. Outliers are data points that differ significantly from other observations and can arise from measurement errors, data entry mistakes, or genuine but rare events. Identifying whether an outlier is an error or a meaningful signal requires both statistical methods and domain knowledge. Depending on the goal of the analysis, outliers might be removed, corrected, or flagged for special treatment. In predictive modeling, especially with machine learning algorithms sensitive to scale and distribution, unhandled outliers can distort results and reduce model performance.

Feature engineering is a sophisticated part of the wrangling process where new variables are created from existing ones to better represent the underlying patterns in the data. This might involve combining columns, extracting substrings, performing mathematical operations, or applying domain-specific transformations. Effective feature engineering can significantly improve model accuracy and interpretability, often making the difference between a mediocre and a high-performing model. It requires creativity, intuition, and a deep understanding of both the data and the business problem being addressed.

Tools play a vital role in streamlining the data wrangling process. Libraries such as Pandas in Python offer powerful functions for manipulating data frames, handling missing values, filtering records, and performing group operations. For larger datasets, tools like Dask or PySpark allow for scalable processing across distributed systems. Visual tools like OpenRefine provide a user-friendly interface for exploring and cleaning data, while Jupyter notebooks allow for documenting and iterating on wrangling steps in an interactive, transparent manner. The choice of tool depends on the size of the data, the complexity of the transformations, and the experience of the practitioner.

Throughout the data wrangling process, documentation is essential. Keeping track of what transformations have been applied, why certain decisions were made, and how data has changed over time ensures that the workflow is reproducible and auditable. This is particularly important when working in teams or in regulated environments where transparency and accountability are crucial. Documenting the process also makes it easier to revisit and refine wrangling steps as new data becomes available or project requirements evolve.

Data wrangling is not a one-time task but a continuous process. As new data sources are introduced, as projects shift direction, or as insights evolve, the data must be revisited and refined. Each iteration brings deeper understanding and improved quality, enhancing the foundation upon which all future analysis rests. Rather than viewing data wrangling as a tedious obligation, skilled data scientists recognize it as a powerful opportunity to engage with their data, uncover hidden patterns, and lay the groundwork for successful discovery. It is during this stage that intuition meets technique, transforming chaotic information into a structured resource ready to yield knowledge.

Cleaning and Preprocessing Raw Data

Cleaning and preprocessing raw data is a vital phase in the data science workflow. Before any analytical model can be built or visualizations created, raw data must be transformed into a state that is clean, consistent, and suitable for analysis. Raw data, by its nature, is often messy and unstructured. It may come from multiple sources, include missing or erroneous values, contain inconsistencies in formatting, or present variables in incompatible scales. Without appropriate preprocessing, any insights derived from such data would be unreliable or even misleading. Therefore, this stage is not only necessary but foundational to all subsequent steps in a data-driven project.

The process begins with a thorough inspection of the dataset to understand its structure, identify inconsistencies, and uncover potential issues. This exploration phase involves looking at data types, summary statistics, unique values, and sample records to gain a sense of the overall quality. In most cases, raw data includes noise in various forms, such as null values, incorrectly typed columns, and redundant features. A key part of the cleaning process is to assess and address these irregularities while preserving as much relevant information as possible. The goal is not merely to sanitize the data but to enhance its usability and reliability.

One of the most common problems in raw datasets is missing data. Missing values can occur for many reasons, such as sensor malfunctions, user input errors, or incomplete records in data collection processes. Addressing missing data requires thoughtful consideration of the context in which the data was collected and the importance of the missing values for the analysis. Simple strategies include removing rows or columns with a high percentage of missing values, but this approach can lead to significant information loss. More sophisticated methods involve imputing missing values using statistical techniques such as mean, median, or mode substitution, or predictive methods like regression and k-nearest neighbors. The choice of method depends on the nature of the data and the extent of the missingness.

In addition to missing values, raw data often contains duplicated records. Duplicates can distort statistical summaries, skew models, and inflate the perceived volume of data. Identifying duplicates typically involves comparing key columns that should uniquely identify a record. Once found, duplicates are either removed entirely or resolved through aggregation or deduplication rules. Ensuring that each observation in a dataset is unique and meaningful is essential for maintaining the integrity of the analysis.

Data type consistency is another key aspect of cleaning. In real-world datasets, especially those compiled from multiple sources, columns may be stored as incorrect types. For example, numerical values might be stored as strings, dates may appear as plain text, or categorical fields could be improperly encoded. Converting data into its appropriate type enables accurate computation and analysis. This might involve parsing date strings into datetime objects, converting string representations of numbers into integers or floats, or mapping categorical variables into standardized labels. Type consistency is not just about technical correctness—it directly affects how functions operate and how models interpret the data.

Outlier detection is also a fundamental part of the cleaning process. Outliers are extreme values that differ significantly from other observations. They can result from data entry errors, unusual but valid events, or measurement anomalies. Detecting outliers often involves statistical techniques, such as using interquartile ranges, standard deviations from the mean, or visual methods like boxplots and scatterplots. The treatment of outliers depends on their cause and the context. They may be corrected, excluded, or left in place if they provide important information. For example, a sudden spike in sales might be an outlier that signals a marketing campaign's success rather than an error.

Text data presents its own unique challenges. Raw text can include inconsistencies in capitalization, punctuation, and spacing, as well as typos, abbreviations, and special characters. Preprocessing text data involves normalization tasks like converting text to lowercase, removing extra whitespace, stripping punctuation, and correcting common misspellings. Tokenization, the process of breaking text into individual words or phrases, is a crucial step before more advanced natural language processing. Depending on the analysis goals, stemming or lemmatization may be used to reduce words to their base or root forms, improving the uniformity of textual representations across the dataset.

Feature scaling and normalization are essential preprocessing steps when working with numerical data, particularly when using algorithms sensitive to variable magnitudes. Features that are measured on different scales can dominate the behavior of machine learning models, especially distance-based ones such as k-nearest neighbors or support vector machines. Scaling ensures that each feature contributes equally by transforming them into a common range, such as through min-max normalization or standardization using z-scores. These techniques align the data distributions, allowing models to focus on patterns rather than differences in scale.

Encoding categorical variables is another crucial task in preprocessing. Most machine learning models cannot work directly with non-numerical inputs, so categorical variables must be transformed into numerical formats. One-hot encoding creates binary columns for each category, which works well for variables with a limited number of values. Label encoding assigns a unique integer to each category but can introduce unintended ordinal relationships. Choosing the right encoding method requires understanding both the algorithm being used and the nature of the categories.

Feature selection and dimensionality reduction are also part of preprocessing. Raw datasets often contain irrelevant or redundant features that add noise and computational overhead without contributing to model performance. Identifying the most informative variables involves statistical tests, correlation analysis, or feature importance scores from model-based approaches. Reducing the dimensionality of the dataset through techniques such as principal component analysis or t-SNE can further improve the performance and interpretability of the model, especially when dealing with high-dimensional data.

Cleaning and preprocessing raw data is not a linear or rigid sequence of steps. It is an iterative, problem-driven process that requires constant adjustment and domain understanding. As the data evolves and insights emerge, previous cleaning decisions may need to be revisited. Effective preprocessing requires attention to detail, technical skill, and a deep appreciation of how data quality influences every aspect of analysis. Through this meticulous work, data scientists convert chaotic, noisy raw inputs into structured, coherent datasets that are ready to support sound, impactful decisions.

Handling Missing and Inconsistent Data

Missing and inconsistent data are two of the most persistent challenges in data science. Regardless of the source or domain, nearly every dataset will present some degree of imperfection. These imperfections can manifest in the form of absent values, conflicting formats, duplicated records, or contradictory entries. If left untreated, such issues can distort statistical summaries, mislead visualizations, and degrade the performance of machine learning models. Effectively addressing missing and inconsistent data is essential for ensuring the quality and reliability of any data-driven analysis. The process demands a combination of statistical reasoning, contextual understanding, and technical fluency in data manipulation tools.

Missing data can occur for various reasons, including system failures, user omissions, data entry errors, or incomplete integrations across systems. In some cases, the data was simply never collected, either by design or oversight. In other cases, values may be masked, anonymized, or redacted due to privacy regulations. Understanding the cause of missing data is critical to choosing the right strategy for handling it. Data can be missing completely at random, missing at random, or missing not at random. Each of these scenarios requires a different approach. When data is missing completely at random, the missingness does not depend on any observed or unobserved data, making it easier to deal with. When data is missing at random, the missingness depends only on observed data and can be handled using more advanced imputation techniques. When it is missing not at random, the mechanism behind the missingness must be modeled explicitly, which adds complexity.

The first step in handling missing data is detection. This involves scanning datasets to identify null values, placeholder values such as zeros or strings like "N/A," or any irregular entries that represent absence. Visualization tools like heatmaps and summary tables can help identify patterns of missingness across variables and records. Once the scope of the problem is known, decisions must be made about how to proceed. Deleting rows or columns with missing values is the simplest approach, but it is only viable when the proportion of missing data is small and its removal does not compromise the integrity of the dataset. In other scenarios, imputing missing values is a better solution.

Imputation refers to the process of filling in missing values using available data. Basic methods include replacing missing values with the mean, median, or mode of the corresponding feature. These approaches are easy to implement and often effective for numerical data with relatively low variance. However, they can distort the distribution of the data and introduce bias if used indiscriminately. More sophisticated imputation methods rely on predictive models. For example, regression-based imputation predicts the missing value of one variable based on the values of others. K-nearest neighbors imputation identifies similar records and estimates missing values from their known features. In time series data, missing values may be filled using forward or backward filling techniques, or interpolated based on temporal patterns. The method chosen must align with the nature of the data and the intended use case, as incorrect imputation can create misleading results and compromise model performance.

Categorical data introduces additional challenges. Missing values in categorical fields can be treated as a separate category, especially when the absence itself carries meaning. Alternatively, they can be imputed based on the most frequent category or using probabilistic models. Care must be taken not to introduce artificial relationships or imbalance class distributions during this process. One useful approach is to create an indicator variable that flags whether a value was originally missing. This preserves information about missingness and allows models to learn from patterns in its occurrence.

Inconsistent data, while different from missing data, often requires similar care and attention. Inconsistencies arise when values that are meant to represent the same information appear in different formats. This includes variations in capitalization, units of measurement, date formats, spelling, or abbreviations. For instance, a country might be represented as "USA," "U.S.," "United States," or "America" within the same dataset. Such inconsistencies hinder grouping, filtering, and aggregation operations and can fragment analytical results. The process of resolving these issues begins with normalization, which standardizes entries to a consistent format. This might involve converting text to lowercase, stripping whitespace, unifying date representations, or mapping synonyms to a single standard term.

Data type mismatches also fall under the umbrella of inconsistency. A numerical field may contain non-numeric strings, or a date field may include invalid entries. These mismatches must be detected and corrected through parsing and coercion functions. Invalid entries can be replaced, converted, or removed depending on the context. In certain cases, inconsistency reveals underlying data quality problems, such as improper data entry processes or merging of incompatible datasets. When merging data from multiple sources, schema mismatches, key collisions, and differing conventions can all introduce inconsistencies that must be reconciled before further analysis can proceed.

In domains with complex hierarchical or relational data, inconsistency can also appear at the structural level. For example, in healthcare data, a patient might have multiple conflicting records for the same visit. In e-commerce, a product might be associated with inconsistent pricing information across different databases. Reconciling such issues requires contextual expertise and often manual intervention. Data scientists must work closely with domain experts to understand which values are authoritative and which should be corrected or discarded. This is particularly important in regulated industries, where the consequences of misinterpreting data can be significant.

Automated validation checks are useful tools for detecting both missing and inconsistent data. These checks enforce rules about acceptable ranges, formats, and relationships between variables. For example, a validation rule might ensure that a date of birth precedes the date of enrollment or that numeric fields fall within a realistic range. Incorporating such checks into the preprocessing pipeline can catch issues early and prevent contaminated data from influencing results. Logging these checks and generating error reports also facilitates communication with data providers and system administrators who can correct issues at the source.

Ultimately, handling missing and inconsistent data is not just a technical exercise. It is a critical step in establishing trust in the dataset and ensuring that downstream analyses are built on a solid foundation. Data scientists must not only clean and standardize the data but also document their decisions, explain their rationale, and consider the implications of each transformation. Transparency in how data quality issues are addressed allows stakeholders to interpret results with confidence and provides a clear audit trail for reproducibility. Whether modeling customer behavior, forecasting demand, or identifying risk factors, the strength of the analysis depends on the rigor with which the data has been prepared. Addressing missing and inconsistent data thoughtfully and systematically enables better decisions, more accurate models, and deeper insight into the phenomena being studied.

Dealing with Outliers and Anomalies

Outliers and anomalies are data points that deviate significantly from the majority of observations in a dataset. They represent rare or extreme values that can arise from various causes such as data entry errors, natural variation, unusual events, or system malfunctions. In many cases, outliers can have a disproportionate impact on statistical summaries, data visualizations, and model predictions. Therefore, identifying and appropriately handling them is a crucial part of the data preprocessing pipeline. The decision on how to treat these anomalies depends heavily on the nature of the dataset, the context in which it was collected, and the goals of the analysis. Ignoring or mishandling outliers can lead to misleading results, distorted patterns, and poor model performance.

The process of dealing with outliers begins with detection. The most straightforward way to identify potential outliers is through visualization. Box plots, scatter plots, and histograms are particularly useful for revealing unusual data points. Box plots, for example, highlight values that lie beyond the interquartile range, giving a quick visual sense of where the extremes fall. Scatter plots are useful for identifying outliers in multivariate data, showing how one variable behaves in relation to another. Visual inspection helps develop an intuitive sense of what is considered normal or abnormal within the data. However, visual tools are often just the starting point, especially in high-dimensional datasets where patterns may not be visible with simple plots.

Statistical methods provide a more systematic approach to outlier detection. One common method is the use of z-scores, which measure how many standard deviations a data point is from the mean. Values with z-scores beyond a certain threshold, such as three, are often considered outliers. Another technique involves the interquartile range (IQR), which defines outliers as values that fall below the first quartile minus 1.5 times the IQR or above the third quartile plus 1.5 times the IQR. These methods are straightforward and effective for detecting univariate outliers but may not capture more subtle or contextual anomalies.

In multivariate datasets, detecting outliers becomes more complex. A data point might appear normal in isolation but be anomalous when all variables are considered together. Techniques such as Mahalanobis distance take into account the correlations between variables and are better suited for identifying multivariate outliers. More advanced algorithms, including isolation forests, one-class support vector machines, and autoencoders, are designed specifically for anomaly detection in high-dimensional spaces. These methods use machine learning to model the distribution of normal data and identify observations that do not conform to the learned patterns. They are particularly useful in large datasets where manual inspection and simple statistical thresholds are insufficient.

Once outliers are detected, the next step is deciding how to handle them. There is no universal rule for dealing with outliers, and the appropriate response depends on whether the anomaly is the result of an error or a legitimate but rare observation. If an outlier is due to a clear error, such as a misplaced decimal point or an incorrect unit of measurement, correction or removal is usually justified. In contrast, if an outlier represents a genuine data point—such as an exceptional sale, an unusual patient response, or a rare event—it may be valuable and should not be discarded lightly. In some cases, these rare observations carry critical information and may even be the focus of the analysis.

Transforming outliers rather than removing them is another option. Applying mathematical transformations, such as logarithms or square roots, can reduce the impact of extreme values and make distributions more symmetrical. Winsorizing, which involves capping extreme values at a specific percentile, is another method used to limit the influence of outliers without discarding data. These approaches help preserve the integrity of the dataset while reducing sensitivity to extreme cases. However, transformations should be applied thoughtfully, as they may obscure meaningful variability or introduce new biases.

Outliers also affect model training and evaluation. Many machine learning algorithms, especially those based on distance calculations or assumptions of normality, are sensitive to extreme values. Linear regression, for example, can be heavily influenced by a single outlier, leading to skewed coefficients and poor generalization. Decision trees and random forests tend to be more robust, as they split data based on thresholds rather than relying on averages. Robust regression techniques, such as RANSAC or Huber regression, are designed to minimize the influence of outliers on the model. Understanding the behavior of different algorithms in the presence of outliers is crucial for selecting the right model and preprocessing strategy.

In the context of anomaly detection, outliers may actually be the target of the analysis rather than a nuisance to be removed. Fraud detection, network intrusion detection, predictive maintenance, and medical diagnostics are all domains where identifying anomalies is the primary goal. In these cases, the challenge is to distinguish between noise and signal, isolating the few critical anomalies from a sea of normal behavior. Building effective anomaly detection models requires labeled data when available, but unsupervised methods are often used due to the rarity and unpredictability of anomalies. Evaluating these models is particularly challenging because traditional accuracy metrics may not reflect true performance when the dataset is heavily imbalanced.

Documentation and transparency are essential when dealing with outliers. Every decision about identifying, transforming, or removing outliers should be recorded, along with the rationale and method used. This documentation ensures reproducibility and allows other team members or stakeholders to understand how the data was handled. It also facilitates future revisions if new data becomes available or if the project goals shift. Transparency builds trust in the results and provides a foundation for sound scientific and business decisions.

Dealing with outliers and anomalies is an iterative process. Initial detection may highlight some issues, but deeper analysis often reveals additional, more subtle anomalies. As data scientists explore and model their data, they must continuously refine their understanding of what constitutes an outlier in that particular context. With each iteration, the data becomes cleaner, more consistent, and better suited to delivering accurate and actionable insights. Outliers are not merely obstacles to be removed—they are opportunities to understand the data more deeply, to question assumptions, and to improve the robustness and reliability of analytical conclusions. Through careful analysis and thoughtful handling, data scientists can navigate the complexity of anomalies and ensure that their models and insights reflect the true nature of the phenomena under investigation.

Data Transformation and Normalization

Data transformation and normalization are critical steps in preparing raw datasets for analysis and modeling. These processes involve modifying the format, structure, or values of data to improve its compatibility with analytical methods, ensure consistency across variables, and enhance the performance of algorithms. As raw data is collected from diverse sources, it often exhibits varying scales, units, distributions, and formats. Without appropriate transformation, these disparities can lead to incorrect interpretations, biased models, and reduced computational efficiency. Transforming and normalizing data brings it into a state where it can be accurately compared, effectively modeled, and meaningfully interpreted.

Data transformation refers to any operation that modifies the data from its original form into a more suitable one. This includes altering variables through arithmetic operations, converting data types, changing formats, and encoding values. One of the most common transformations is the application of mathematical functions to numerical features. Logarithmic, square root, exponential, and polynomial transformations are frequently used to modify distributions, stabilize variance, or linearize relationships between variables. For example, right-skewed data with heavy tails, such as income or population sizes, can be transformed using a logarithmic function to compress extreme values and bring the distribution closer to normality, which is a common assumption in many statistical models.

Normalization, a specific type of transformation, involves adjusting the scale of numerical values so that they fall within a defined range or distribution. This is especially important when working with machine learning algorithms that are sensitive to the magnitude of input features. Algorithms like k-nearest neighbors, support vector machines, and gradient descent-based models are affected by the relative scales of variables, which can cause features with larger values to dominate the learning process. Normalization ensures that each feature contributes equally by bringing all variables to a comparable scale. Two widely used normalization techniques are min-max scaling and z-score standardization.

Min-max scaling transforms data to a fixed range, typically between zero and one. This technique subtracts the minimum value from each data point and then divides by the range of the data. While effective in maintaining the relationships between values, min-max scaling is sensitive to outliers. A single extreme value can significantly distort the scale, compressing the majority of data into a narrow band. To mitigate this, it is often combined with outlier handling techniques before normalization is applied.

Z-score standardization, also known as standard scaling, transforms data by subtracting the mean and dividing by the standard deviation. This results in a distribution with a mean of zero and a standard deviation of one. Z-score standardization is more robust to outliers than min-max scaling and is preferred when the data follows or approximates a normal distribution. It is especially useful in contexts where the interpretability of the standardized scores, such as how many standard deviations a value is from the mean, provides analytical value.

Beyond numerical scaling, data transformation includes the encoding of categorical variables, which is essential for integrating non-numeric data into machine learning models. Most algorithms require inputs to be numerical, so textual or categorical data must be converted. One-hot encoding creates binary columns for each category, marking the presence of a particular class with a one and the absence with a zero. While effective, this can lead to high-dimensional datasets if a categorical variable contains many unique values. Label encoding assigns a unique integer to each category, but it introduces an artificial ordinal relationship that may mislead algorithms. More sophisticated techniques, like target encoding or embedding representations, can be used to preserve complex relationships in categorical data without inflating dimensionality.

Datetime transformations are another critical area of data preprocessing. Raw datetime fields often contain rich information that must be extracted to be useful. Features such as year, month, day of the week, hour, or even holidays and seasons can be derived from a single datetime column. These derived features help capture temporal patterns and trends. Additionally, time deltas, or differences between two timestamps, are commonly used in event-based datasets to measure durations, intervals, or lag effects.

Normalization and transformation are also vital in dealing with data distributions that violate the assumptions of analytical models. Many statistical and machine learning methods assume linearity, normality, or homoscedasticity in the data. When these assumptions are violated, the results can be invalid or suboptimal. Transformations like Box-Cox or Yeo-Johnson are designed to automatically find a power transformation that stabilizes variance and brings data closer to a normal distribution. These methods are particularly useful in regression modeling, where residual diagnostics can reveal the need for transformation to meet model assumptions.

Feature scaling also plays an important role in dimensionality reduction techniques such as principal component analysis. These techniques are sensitive to the variance of input features, and unscaled data can result in biased projections where features with larger magnitudes dominate the analysis. Properly scaled data ensures that each variable contributes equally to the reduced dimensions, allowing for more accurate and interpretable components.

In some cases, transformations are applied to enhance interpretability rather than model performance. For example, converting bytes to megabytes or milliseconds to seconds makes data more comprehensible to humans. Log transformations are frequently used in visualizations to better represent data that spans several orders of magnitude. These transformations do not change the underlying data relationships but make patterns easier to see and communicate.

Data transformation must always be guided by domain knowledge and the specific objectives of the analysis. Arbitrary transformations can obscure meaningful relationships or introduce artifacts that mislead interpretation. Understanding the underlying data, its source, and its role in the analysis is essential to choosing appropriate transformation strategies. Additionally, transformation steps should be carefully documented and reproducible. In production environments, consistent application of the same transformations during model training and prediction is critical for maintaining accuracy.

Transforming and normalizing data is not a one-size-fits-all process. It requires experimentation, iteration, and critical thinking. As the dataset evolves or as new features are added, transformation strategies may need to be revisited and revised. What works for one algorithm or problem type may not be appropriate for another. Ultimately, the effectiveness of data transformation and normalization is reflected in the quality and reliability of the final model. These preprocessing steps allow the data to speak more clearly, revealing patterns and structures that might otherwise remain hidden behind inconsistencies and noise. Through thoughtful transformation, data becomes more than raw material—it becomes a refined input, ready to fuel robust and insightful analysis.

Exploratory Data Analysis Fundamentals

Exploratory Data Analysis, often abbreviated as EDA, is a fundamental phase in any data science project. It serves as the bridge between raw data and modeling, allowing analysts and data scientists to understand the underlying structure, detect anomalies, identify patterns, and generate hypotheses. EDA is not simply a procedural task; it is a dynamic and iterative process of inquiry, experimentation, and interpretation. Through this process, one begins to develop a deep familiarity with the dataset, uncovering its strengths, weaknesses, and potential for driving actionable insights.

The primary goal of exploratory data analysis is to gain an intuitive and comprehensive understanding of the data before applying any formal statistical models or machine learning algorithms. This understanding begins with examining the basic properties of the dataset, including its shape, types of variables, and summary statistics. A data scientist typically starts by checking the number of observations and features, identifying data types such as numerical, categorical, or datetime, and reviewing the completeness of the dataset. Measures of central tendency like mean and median, and measures of spread such as standard deviation, range, and interquartile range, provide a high-level overview of how each variable behaves.

Beyond numerical summaries, visual exploration plays a central role in EDA. Visualization allows for the detection of patterns, trends, and relationships that might not be evident through numbers alone. For example, histograms reveal the distribution of a single variable, showing whether it is symmetric, skewed, or multimodal. Boxplots highlight the presence of outliers and the spread of data within and across categories. Scatter plots display relationships between two continuous variables, indicating linearity, clusters, or potential correlations. Pair plots or correlation heatmaps help uncover interdependencies among multiple variables, guiding further investigation into predictive relationships or multicollinearity.

EDA is also where data quality issues become apparent. Missing values, inconsistent formats, duplicate records, and outliers often reveal themselves during this phase. Identifying these problems early is essential because they can distort analytical results and affect the performance of predictive models. For instance, an unexpected spike in a histogram may suggest a data entry error, while gaps in a time series might point to system failures or periods of inactivity. Exploratory analysis thus serves both as a diagnostic tool and a method of quality assurance, ensuring that the dataset is suitable for deeper analysis.

Understanding the nature of variables is another key component of EDA. Numerical variables can be continuous or discrete, and their treatment depends on their statistical properties and the distribution they follow. Skewed distributions may require transformations such as logarithmic scaling to achieve normality, which is often desirable for many statistical techniques. Categorical variables, on the other hand, are explored by counting frequencies, examining proportions, and comparing distributions across different groups. Bar charts, pie charts, and count plots are typical tools for visualizing these variables. When categorical variables have an inherent order, such as educational attainment or income brackets, the analysis must account for that ordinality to avoid misinterpretation.

The relationships between variables are at the heart of exploratory analysis. Investigating how one variable affects or correlates with another is critical for building predictive models and generating insights. Correlation coefficients, such as Pearson or Spearman, provide numerical measures of linear or monotonic associations. However, correlation does not imply causation, and visual methods often reveal more nuanced relationships. For example, a scatter plot may show a curved pattern that is not captured by a simple correlation coefficient. Grouped boxplots can illustrate how a numerical variable differs across levels of a categorical variable, offering hints about potential predictors and interactions.

EDA also involves segmenting the data into meaningful subgroups. By stratifying the data based on attributes such as age, region, gender, or product category, analysts can compare patterns across groups and detect hidden trends. This stratified analysis helps avoid misleading generalizations and highlights heterogeneity within the dataset. For instance, overall sales might appear stable, but a breakdown by region could reveal a decline in one area and growth in another. Segmenting data in this way supports better business decisions and more targeted interventions.

Time-based data introduces its own set of exploratory techniques. When dealing with time series, it is essential to examine seasonality, trends, and autocorrelation. Line plots are commonly used to visualize temporal patterns, making it easier to detect cycles, abrupt changes, or missing periods. Lag plots and autocorrelation functions help evaluate the relationship between observations over time, guiding the choice of models for forecasting and temporal prediction. Understanding the temporal structure of the data is vital for accurate modeling and ensuring that future values are predictable based on past behavior.

The EDA process also benefits from domain knowledge. Contextual understanding helps interpret the patterns and anomalies revealed during exploration. For example, a spike in web traffic might be expected during a holiday season or a product launch. Conversely, a dip in performance metrics could be explained by external events such as economic downturns or supply chain disruptions. Without domain insight, EDA risks becoming a purely mechanical exercise, disconnected from the realities of the business or scientific questions at hand.

Automation can assist in the EDA process, but it cannot replace the human intuition and curiosity that drive exploration. Tools like Pandas Profiling, Sweetviz, and AutoViz can generate comprehensive reports, including summary statistics, correlation matrices, and visualizations. These tools are useful for quickly surfacing key characteristics of the dataset. However, true understanding comes from interacting with the data directly, asking questions, testing hypotheses, and following the leads uncovered during exploration. Each dataset has its own story, and EDA is the process of discovering and understanding that narrative.

Exploratory Data Analysis is not a one-time step but an iterative cycle that continues throughout the data science workflow. As new data is collected, as modeling decisions are made, and as results are interpreted, analysts often return to EDA to revisit assumptions, refine feature engineering, or probe unexpected model behavior. The depth and thoroughness of EDA often determine the success of the entire project. It lays the groundwork for modeling, shapes the understanding of the problem space, and provides the confidence that the patterns observed are grounded in real data. Through EDA, data scientists develop the insight and intuition necessary to turn raw data into meaningful, actionable knowledge.

Statistical Measures and Their Interpretations

Statistical measures form the backbone of data analysis. They provide a structured way to summarize, describe, and interpret large quantities of data, allowing patterns and trends to emerge from what would otherwise be overwhelming complexity. These measures are essential in every stage of data science, from exploratory data analysis to model validation. Understanding what each measure represents, how it is calculated, and how it should be interpreted in context enables data scientists to extract meaningful insights and make informed decisions.

The application of statistical measures transforms raw numbers into knowledge, offering a language for describing uncertainty, variation, and structure within a dataset.

One of the most fundamental statistical concepts is the measure of central tendency. Central tendency refers to the typical or central value around which the data tends to cluster. The mean, median, and mode are the primary measures in this category. The mean, or arithmetic average, is calculated by summing all values and dividing by the number of observations. It is widely used due to its mathematical properties, but it is highly sensitive to outliers. The median, on the other hand, represents the middle value when data is ordered, and is more robust in the presence of extreme values. In skewed distributions, the median provides a better indication of central location than the mean. The mode identifies the most frequently occurring value in the dataset and is particularly useful for categorical data, where other measures of central tendency are not applicable.

Complementing central tendency are measures of dispersion, which describe the spread or variability within a dataset. The most common of these are the range, variance, and standard deviation. The range is the simplest measure, calculated as the difference between the maximum and minimum values. While easy to compute, it is highly sensitive to outliers and does not provide information about the distribution between the extremes. Variance measures the average squared deviation from the mean, offering a sense of how much the data varies on average. Standard deviation, the square root of variance, brings the measure back to the original units of the data, making it easier to interpret. A small standard deviation indicates that data points are clustered closely around the mean, while a large standard deviation suggests widespread dispersion.

Another useful set of statistical tools are percentiles and quartiles, which divide data into intervals and help describe its distribution. The 25th, 50th, and 75th percentiles correspond to the first, second, and third quartiles, respectively. The difference between the third and first quartile is known as the interquartile range, a robust measure of dispersion that is less affected by outliers. Percentiles are particularly valuable when comparing an individual value to a population, as they indicate the percentage of data points below a given value. For example, a score in the 90th percentile is higher than 90 percent of all other scores, providing a relative measure of performance or standing.

Statistical measures also include indicators of shape, such as skewness and kurtosis. Skewness measures the asymmetry of the distribution. A positive skew indicates a longer right tail, where most values are concentrated on the left but a few large values pull the mean to the right. A negative skew suggests the opposite, with a long tail on the left. Understanding skewness is crucial when selecting the appropriate measures of central tendency and when interpreting data visualizations. Kurtosis, on the other hand, assesses the heaviness of the tails in a distribution. High kurtosis indicates more frequent extreme deviations from the mean, while low kurtosis suggests a flatter distribution. These shape descriptors help identify non-normal distributions and potential data quality issues.

In inferential statistics, measures such as standard error, confidence intervals, and p-values come into play. The standard error quantifies the variability of a sample statistic, such as the sample mean, from the true population parameter. It decreases as sample size increases, reflecting the greater stability of estimates based on more data. Confidence intervals provide a range of values within which the true population parameter is likely to fall, given a certain level of confidence. For instance, a 95 percent confidence interval implies that if the same experiment were repeated many times, the interval would contain the true value in 95 out of 100 cases. P-values assess the strength of evidence against a null hypothesis. A small p-value suggests that the observed data is unlikely under the assumption of the null hypothesis, prompting consideration of an alternative hypothesis. While widely used, p-values must be interpreted carefully, as they do not measure the probability that a hypothesis is true and are highly sensitive to sample size and study design.

Correlation and covariance are statistical measures that describe the relationship between two variables. Covariance indicates the direction of the relationship: a positive covariance means the variables tend to increase together, while a negative value implies one decreases as the other increases. However, because covariance is not standardized, it is difficult to interpret its magnitude across different datasets. Correlation, particularly Pearson's correlation coefficient, standardizes the measure by dividing covariance by the product of the standard deviations of the two variables. This results in a value between -1 and 1, where -1 indicates a perfect negative linear relationship, 0 implies no linear relationship, and 1 signifies a perfect positive linear relationship. Understanding these measures is essential when evaluating multicollinearity, selecting features, or interpreting relationships in data visualizations.

Another important category includes categorical data measures such as frequency counts, proportions, and contingency tables. Frequency counts show how often each category occurs in a dataset, while proportions express these counts relative to the total. Contingency tables display the frequency distribution of variables across different categories, allowing for the analysis of relationships between categorical variables. Chi-square tests are often used in conjunction with contingency tables to assess whether observed frequencies differ significantly from expected frequencies under the assumption of independence.

Effect sizes are statistical measures that describe the magnitude of a relationship or difference, independent of sample size. Common examples include Cohen's d, which quantifies the difference between two means in terms of standard deviation, and odds ratios or risk ratios in categorical data analysis. Effect sizes complement p-values by providing information about practical significance, helping analysts determine whether an observed effect is not only statistically significant but also meaningful in context.

Understanding statistical measures and their interpretations allows data scientists to navigate the complexities of real-world data with confidence. These measures are not abstract calculations but tools that provide clarity, structure, and depth to analysis. They guide decisions, shape narratives, and reveal the underlying truths hidden within datasets. Mastery of these concepts empowers practitioners to move beyond surface-level summaries and engage deeply with data, leading to more accurate models, better decisions, and richer insights.

Visualizing Data for Insights

Data visualization is an essential aspect of the data science process, transforming raw numbers into meaningful visuals that communicate patterns, trends, and relationships with clarity and impact. It is through visualization that data becomes accessible not only to analysts and scientists but also to business stakeholders, policymakers, and general audiences. Effective visualization bridges the gap between complex analysis and decision-making, allowing insights to emerge in a form that is immediately graspable. The process of visualizing data is not merely about creating aesthetically pleasing graphics but about choosing the most appropriate representation to uncover insights, highlight anomalies, and support storytelling grounded in evidence.

At its core, data visualization is about encoding information visually in a way that leverages human perception. Our brains are wired to recognize shapes, patterns, and colors more efficiently than abstract numbers. When data is presented in a visual format, such as a bar chart or scatter plot, the observer can quickly identify trends, detect outliers, compare values, and understand distributions. The choice of visualization depends on the nature of the data and the question being asked. Each type of chart or graph offers a unique perspective, and the effectiveness of a visualization depends on how well it aligns with the data structure and the analytical objective.

Univariate visualizations are used to explore the distribution of a single variable. Histograms are ideal for examining the frequency distribution of numerical data, revealing the shape of the distribution, such as whether it is symmetric, skewed, or multimodal. Bar charts serve a similar purpose for categorical data, showing the count or proportion of observations in each category. These visualizations are fundamental for detecting data quality issues such as unexpected values, gaps, or overrepresented categories. They also help in deciding which transformations may be necessary before modeling.

Bivariate and multivariate visualizations provide deeper insights into relationships between two or more variables. Scatter plots are one of the most commonly used tools for identifying correlations, clusters, or non-linear relationships between numerical variables. Adding a regression line or color gradient can enhance the ability to detect trends or segment patterns. Box plots are useful for comparing distributions across categories, highlighting medians, quartiles, and potential outliers. They offer a compact and information-rich view of group differences and variability. For time series data, line charts are the go-to visualization, as they effectively show changes over time and help in identifying trends, seasonality, and irregular fluctuations.

When visualizing more complex datasets, advanced visualizations such as heatmaps, pair plots, and bubble charts become valuable. Heatmaps, which use color to represent values in a matrix, are especially helpful in visualizing correlation matrices or hierarchical clustering results. Pair plots, which display scatter plots for each pair of variables in a dataset, allow for the exploration of multidimensional relationships. Bubble charts extend scatter plots by incorporating a third variable through the size of the bubbles, enabling the comparison of three variables simultaneously. These tools allow for rich, multi-layered analysis that can reveal subtle interactions and associations.

Interactivity adds another dimension to data visualization, particularly in exploratory analysis and dashboards. Interactive visualizations allow users to zoom, filter, and hover over data points to reveal additional information. This enables a more dynamic exploration of the data, where users can ask questions and receive immediate feedback. Tools such as Plotly, Tableau, Power BI, and interactive JavaScript libraries like D3.js empower analysts to create visualizations that are not only informative but also engaging. Interactivity enhances understanding by allowing users to tailor the view to their specific interests, dive deeper into subsets of data, and generate new hypotheses in real time.

Good visualization also adheres to principles of clarity and simplicity. It avoids clutter, redundant elements, and misleading scales that can distort interpretation. Axes should be clearly labeled, legends should be easy to understand, and colors should be used consistently and meaningfully. Choosing the right scale, such as linear or logarithmic, can dramatically affect how a trend is perceived. Color palettes must be accessible to individuals with color vision deficiencies and should enhance rather than obscure the data. Annotation is another critical component. Well-placed text and markers can draw attention to key data points, explain anomalies, or summarize trends, guiding the viewer through the narrative the data is telling.

Contextual awareness is key when designing visualizations. A visualization that is appropriate for technical analysis might be overwhelming or confusing for a non-technical audience. For example, a stakeholder presentation may benefit from simplified charts that emphasize key takeaways, whereas an internal data exploration session might involve dense plots that reveal underlying complexity. Understanding the audience and tailoring the visual message accordingly ensures that insights are communicated effectively. In business environments, decision-makers rely on clear visual evidence to drive strategic choices, and in research, compelling visuals can highlight the significance of results and foster understanding across disciplines.

Data storytelling merges visualization with narrative to create a compelling case built on data. This approach involves structuring a sequence of visuals that build upon one another to convey a message, often supported by text, annotations, and contextual cues. The aim is not only to show what the data reveals but to guide the audience through a logical journey that leads to a clear understanding or decision. Data storytelling is particularly powerful when combined with interactivity, allowing users to explore the story from multiple perspectives and arrive at insights through their own engagement with the data.

While visualization can powerfully illuminate data, it can also mislead if used improperly. Cherry-picking data, truncating axes, or using inappropriate chart types can create deceptive impressions. Ethical visualization practices are essential, especially when communicating findings to a broad or influential audience. Transparency about data sources, methods, and limitations reinforces trust and encourages responsible interpretation. Data scientists and analysts bear the responsibility of presenting information honestly, ensuring that the visuals support accurate conclusions rather than distort them.

In modern data science, the ability to visualize data is not an optional skill but a core competency. It enhances every stage of the analytical workflow, from initial exploration to final communication. It enables collaboration across roles and disciplines, bridging the gap between raw data and actionable understanding. Through visualization, data scientists not only uncover insights but also make those insights accessible, persuasive, and impactful. Whether designing an executive dashboard, building a research report, or exploring a new dataset, visualization is the lens through which data becomes knowledge and knowledge becomes action.

Feature Engineering Techniques

Feature engineering is one of the most crucial stages in the data science pipeline, often determining the success or failure of a predictive model. It involves the creation, transformation, and selection of variables—or features—that best represent the underlying problem and facilitate effective learning by algorithms. While raw data can contain valuable signals, those signals are rarely accessible in their original form. Feature engineering unlocks these hidden patterns by reshaping the data into a structure that enhances the model's ability to detect relationships, capture variation, and make accurate predictions. It is both an art and a science, requiring creativity, domain knowledge, and technical skill.

At its core, feature engineering is about extracting meaningful information from raw data. This can involve generating new features, modifying existing ones, or encoding complex structures in a way that models can interpret. One of the simplest yet most effective techniques is polynomial transformation, where new features are created by raising existing features to a power or multiplying them together. This can help capture non-linear relationships that a linear model might otherwise miss. For instance, if the target variable increases with the square of an input, creating a squared term allows the model to align more closely with the true function. Interaction terms between features can also reveal combined effects that would not be apparent when features are considered in isolation.

Temporal data opens up additional avenues for feature engineering. When working with time-stamped records, extracting features such as day of the week, hour of the day, or whether a date falls on a weekend or holiday can provide valuable context. Lag features, which incorporate values from previous time steps, are essential in time series forecasting. Rolling statistics, such as moving averages or exponentially weighted means, help smooth out noise and highlight trends. Duration-based features, which measure the time between events, can provide insight into user behavior or system performance. These temporal transformations help capture dynamics over time and support models that depend on the order or frequency of events.

Text data requires a specialized set of feature engineering techniques. Raw text cannot be used directly in most machine learning models and must be transformed into numerical representations. One common method is the bag-of-words approach, which counts the frequency of each word in a document and treats each count as a separate feature. While simple, this method often results in high-dimensional and sparse data. Term frequency-inverse document frequency (TF-IDF) improves upon this by weighting terms based on how unique they are across all documents, emphasizing words that carry more informational value. More advanced techniques include word embeddings like Word2Vec or GloVe, which map words into dense vectors that capture semantic similarity. These representations can be averaged, concatenated, or passed through recurrent neural networks for further modeling.

Categorical variables also require careful treatment. Label encoding converts categories into integers, but this can introduce unintended ordinal relationships that mislead certain models. One-hot encoding addresses this by creating binary indicators for each category, which works well for variables with a limited number of levels. However, when a categorical feature has many unique values, such as zip codes or product IDs, one-hot encoding becomes inefficient and can lead to sparse data. In such cases, techniques like target encoding or frequency encoding offer alternatives. Target encoding replaces each category with the average of the target variable for that category, which can capture meaningful patterns but must be applied carefully to avoid overfitting.

Numerical features can often benefit from normalization or standardization. These transformations ensure that features are on a comparable scale, which is particularly important for distance-based algorithms like k-nearest neighbors or gradient-based optimization methods. Logarithmic transformations help compress right-skewed distributions, making them more symmetric and reducing the impact of extreme values. Binning or discretization can be used to convert continuous variables into categorical ones, which may help models identify threshold effects or simplify interactions. Quantile-based binning ensures that each bin contains approximately the same number of observations, preserving the distribution while reducing granularity.

Missing data presents another opportunity for feature engineering. Rather than simply imputing missing values, one can create binary indicators that flag the presence or absence of data. This can reveal patterns in the missingness itself, which might correlate with the target variable. In some contexts, the fact that a value is missing is itself informative. For example, if income is missing more often for a certain group of users, that absence may reflect a broader behavioral pattern. Including such indicators allows models to take advantage of this implicit signal.

Feature selection is a closely related discipline that involves choosing which features to include in a model. Not all engineered features will contribute to better performance, and some may introduce noise or redundancy. Methods for feature selection range from simple techniques like removing features with low variance or high correlation, to more sophisticated methods like recursive feature elimination, mutual information scores, and regularization techniques such as Lasso. Feature importance scores from tree-based models can also guide selection by ranking features based on their contribution to predictive accuracy. Pruning the feature set helps prevent overfitting, reduces computational complexity, and improves interpretability.

Another powerful concept in feature engineering is dimensionality reduction. Techniques like principal component analysis reduce the number of features while preserving as much variance as possible. This can be especially useful when dealing with high-dimensional data, where too many features can dilute the signal and slow down processing. Dimensionality reduction techniques transform the original features into new, uncorrelated components, which can sometimes reveal latent structure in the data. While interpretability may be reduced, these techniques often enhance model performance and stability.

Automated feature engineering tools and libraries are increasingly available to assist in the process, but human intuition remains irreplaceable. Tools like Featuretools can generate large sets of candidate features through predefined operations, especially in relational or time-indexed datasets. However, the most impactful features often arise from domain-specific insights. Understanding the business context, the problem being solved, and the behavior of the system or users being modeled allows for the creation of features that truly capture the essence of the task.

Feature engineering is iterative by nature. As models are trained and evaluated, their performance informs which features are effective and which need refinement. Unexpected results, such as overfitting or poor generalization, often trace back to poorly constructed or overly complex features. Re-examining the data, trying new transformations, or combining features in novel ways can unlock significant improvements. In many real-world projects, feature engineering is not a separate stage but a continuous process of exploration, hypothesis, testing, and refinement. It is where data science blends technical acumen with creative problem-solving, producing the representations that turn raw data into predictive power.

Dimensionality Reduction Methods

Dimensionality reduction is a critical technique in data science, particularly when working with datasets that contain a large number of features. High-dimensional data can pose several challenges, such as increased computational cost, difficulty in visualization, and the risk of overfitting. As the number of features increases, the volume of the feature space grows exponentially, which leads to a phenomenon known as the curse of dimensionality. In such scenarios, data points become sparse and models struggle to generalize because the distance between observations becomes less meaningful. Dimensionality reduction aims to address these issues by transforming high-dimensional data into a lower-dimensional representation while preserving as much of the original structure and information as possible.

There are two primary goals of dimensionality reduction. One is to improve model performance by eliminating redundant or irrelevant features that add noise rather than useful signal. The other is to enable more effective data visualization by projecting data into two or three dimensions, making it easier to observe patterns, trends, and groupings. By reducing the number of input variables, dimensionality reduction can also simplify the interpretation of models, enhance training speed, and reduce the memory footprint of data storage and processing.

One of the most widely used techniques for dimensionality reduction is Principal Component Analysis, or PCA. PCA is a linear transformation method that identifies the directions, known as principal components, along which the variance of the data is maximized. These principal components are orthogonal to each other, ensuring that they capture different aspects of the data. PCA begins by centering the data, subtracting the mean from each feature. It then computes the covariance matrix and derives its eigenvalues and eigenvectors. The eigenvectors define the new axes of the transformed space, and the corresponding eigenvalues indicate the amount of variance captured by each principal component. By selecting the top components that explain most of the variance, one can reduce the dimensionality of the data while retaining its most significant characteristics.

PCA is especially effective when the data has a lot of correlated features. In such cases, a few principal components can often explain a large portion of the total variance, allowing for a substantial reduction in dimensionality with minimal loss of information. However, PCA assumes linear relationships between features and may not perform well when the data contains complex, nonlinear structures. Additionally, the transformed features produced by PCA are linear combinations of the original variables, which can make interpretation difficult, especially in domains where explainability is important.

Another technique for dimensionality reduction is t-distributed Stochastic Neighbor Embedding, or t-SNE. Unlike PCA, which is a linear method, t-SNE is a nonlinear technique that focuses on preserving the local structure of the data. It is particularly effective for visualizing high-dimensional data in two or three dimensions. t-SNE works by modeling the probability distribution of pairs of points in the high-dimensional space and then finding a lower-dimensional embedding that best preserves these pairwise similarities. It emphasizes maintaining the relative distances of nearby points while de-emphasizing the distances between faraway points.

t-SNE is widely used in exploratory data analysis, especially in fields like genomics, natural language processing, and image recognition, where data is often high-dimensional and structured in complex ways. However, it has limitations. It is computationally intensive and does not scale well to very large datasets. It is also sensitive to hyperparameters such as perplexity and learning rate, which must be carefully tuned to produce meaningful visualizations. Furthermore, t-SNE is not ideal for preserving global structure or for use as a preprocessing step for supervised learning, as the resulting embeddings are not deterministic or consistent across different runs.

A similar but more scalable nonlinear method is Uniform Manifold Approximation and Projection, or UMAP. UMAP builds upon mathematical concepts from topology and manifold theory to construct a graph of the data in high-dimensional space and then optimizes a low-dimensional projection that preserves both local and global structure. It offers faster computation and better scalability than t-SNE, along with improved preservation of the data's topological structure. UMAP has become popular in recent years for both visualization and as a preprocessing step for clustering or classification algorithms.

In addition to these projection-based methods, there are feature selection techniques that reduce dimensionality by selecting a subset of the original variables rather than transforming them. Methods like recursive feature elimination, mutual information scores, and model-based importance rankings can identify which features are most informative for the target variable. Unlike PCA or t-SNE, these methods preserve the original feature names and meanings, which can be important in applications where interpretability is crucial.

Autoencoders offer another approach to dimensionality reduction, especially in deep learning contexts. An autoencoder is a type of neural network trained to reconstruct its input. It consists of an encoder, which compresses the input into a lower-dimensional latent space, and a decoder, which attempts to reconstruct the original input from this compressed representation. The bottleneck layer in the middle of the network captures the essential structure of the data. Once trained, the encoder portion of the autoencoder can be used to transform data into a lower-dimensional space for visualization, clustering, or as input to other machine learning models. Autoencoders are highly flexible and capable of capturing complex nonlinear relationships, but they require careful tuning and large amounts of data for effective training.

When applying dimensionality reduction, it is important to evaluate the trade-offs between information loss and model performance. Retaining too few dimensions may discard valuable information, while keeping too many may negate the benefits of simplification. Techniques such as explained variance in PCA or reconstruction error in autoencoders can help guide the choice of the number of dimensions to retain. Additionally, it is crucial to consider the downstream application of the reduced data. For instance, if the reduced features will be used in supervised learning, it is important to ensure that the transformation preserves information relevant to the target variable.

Dimensionality reduction is not a one-size-fits-all solution. Different methods are suited to different types of data and analysis goals. The choice between linear and nonlinear methods, between projection and selection, and between interpretable and abstract features depends on the context and constraints of the problem. Mastering these techniques allows data scientists to tame high-dimensional data, uncover hidden patterns, and build models that are both efficient and effective. It empowers them to move beyond the limitations of raw data and harness the full potential of the information it contains.

Encoding Categorical Variables

Encoding categorical variables is a fundamental step in preparing data for machine learning and statistical modeling. Most algorithms are designed to work with numerical inputs, and as such, non-numeric features must be transformed into a format that these algorithms can understand and process. Categorical variables are those that represent discrete groups or labels, such as gender, occupation, city, or product category. These variables carry important information that can significantly influence predictions, but in their raw form, they cannot be directly utilized by most models. Therefore, encoding these variables into numerical representations becomes essential to extract their predictive power while maintaining the integrity of the data.

The simplest method for encoding categorical variables is label encoding. This technique assigns a unique integer to each category within a feature. For instance, the variable representing color with values like red, blue, and green might be encoded as 0, 1, and 2 respectively. Label encoding is straightforward and efficient, especially when dealing with ordinal variables, which have an inherent order. For example, education levels such as high school, bachelor's, master's, and PhD can be represented numerically in a way that preserves their hierarchy. However, label encoding can introduce unintended ordinal relationships when applied to nominal variables, where the categories have no logical order. Treating unordered categories as if they are ranked can mislead algorithms, especially those sensitive to numerical distance, such as linear regression or k-nearest neighbors.

To address the limitations of label encoding for nominal data, one-hot encoding is widely used. This technique creates a new binary column for each category, assigning a value of one to the corresponding category and zero to all others. If a variable has four unique categories, four new columns are created, each representing the presence or absence of one category. One-hot encoding effectively eliminates any implied order among the categories and ensures that each is treated independently by the model. It is particularly effective for tree-based models and algorithms that do not assume a numerical relationship between features. However, one-hot encoding can lead to a dramatic increase in the dimensionality of the dataset, especially when dealing with features that have a large number of unique values. This sparsity can lead to increased memory usage and slower training times.

To mitigate the issue of high cardinality in categorical variables, frequency encoding and target encoding are alternative approaches. Frequency encoding replaces each category with the frequency or count of its occurrence in the dataset. This approach is simple, compact, and often effective for reducing dimensionality while retaining useful information. However, it can introduce bias if the frequency correlates with the target variable in a way that inflates its importance. Target encoding goes a step further by replacing each category with the mean of the target variable for that category. For example, in a regression problem, each category could be encoded with the average value of the target variable among all instances with that category. This technique captures the direct relationship between the category and the outcome, often improving model performance. Still, it must be used carefully to avoid overfitting, especially when applied to small datasets. Regularization techniques and cross-validation can help mitigate these risks by smoothing the target encoding and preventing leakage of target information.

Another method that has gained popularity, particularly in the context of gradient boosting frameworks, is ordinal encoding with smoothing. This technique orders categories based on their relationship with the target and applies a form of regularization to reduce the impact of rare categories. It provides a balance between simplicity and effectiveness, preserving some of the benefits of target encoding while reducing the risk of overfitting. In addition to these numerical methods, entity embedding is a more advanced approach that uses neural networks to learn dense vector representations of categories. Originally developed for use in deep learning architectures, embeddings can capture complex relationships between categories in a low-dimensional space. These learned vectors can then be used as inputs to other models, combining the interpretability of engineered features with the flexibility of neural representations.

When choosing an encoding method, it is important to consider the model being used. Linear models often perform better with one-hot encoding, as it avoids introducing false assumptions about the relationships between categories. Tree-based models, such as decision trees and random forests, are more robust to label encoding and can naturally handle categorical splits, though they can also benefit from frequency or target encoding. In deep learning models, embeddings tend to outperform traditional encoding methods by capturing rich representations that generalize well to unseen data. The choice of encoding strategy should also take into account the size of the dataset, the cardinality of the categorical variables, and the interpretability requirements of the application.

Interpretability is a key concern in many domains, such as finance, healthcare, and law, where decisions need to be explained and justified. In such cases, encoding methods that preserve the transparency of the original categories are preferred. One-hot encoding and label encoding are generally more interpretable because they maintain a direct correspondence with the original labels. More complex methods like target encoding or embeddings, while often more powerful, can obscure the relationship between input features and predictions. In regulated environments or high-stakes applications, the trade-off between performance and transparency must be carefully managed.

Encoding categorical variables is not merely a technical requirement but a strategic decision that can shape the outcome of a machine learning project. Poor encoding choices can distort relationships, inflate model complexity, and reduce predictive accuracy. Conversely, well-designed encoding strategies can enhance model performance, improve generalization, and reveal new insights hidden in the categorical data. It is an iterative process that benefits from experimentation, validation, and a deep understanding of both the data and the models involved. By treating encoding as an integral part of feature engineering rather than a mechanical step, data scientists can unlock the full potential of categorical variables and build models that are both robust and meaningful.

Time Series Data Preparation

Time series data presents a unique set of challenges and opportunities in the field of data science. Unlike standard datasets where observations are assumed to be independent and identically distributed, time series data is inherently sequential and temporally dependent. Each data point is not just a measurement; it is a measurement anchored in time, and the order in which observations occur holds critical information. Preparing time series data for analysis or modeling requires a distinct approach that respects its temporal structure and ensures the integrity of time-based patterns. Effective preparation is essential for forecasting, anomaly detection, and understanding trends, seasonality, and cyclic behavior.

The first step in time series data preparation involves parsing and standardizing timestamps. In many datasets, time-related data may be stored as strings or in inconsistent formats. Converting these into proper datetime objects is necessary to allow for accurate time-based indexing and manipulation. Once standardized, timestamps must be set as the index of the data frame if the analytical tools in use rely on time-aware indexing. This step enables resampling, rolling calculations, and time-based filtering, which are fundamental operations in time series analysis. Attention must also be paid to time zones, especially when data is collected across different regions. Misalignment in time zones can lead to misinterpretation of temporal trends or errors in synchronization when merging datasets.

Regularity of time intervals is another critical factor. Time series models often assume that observations occur at consistent intervals, whether hourly, daily, weekly, or monthly. However, real-world data frequently includes missing timestamps, irregular gaps, or duplicate records. Resampling is a technique used to convert data into a uniform frequency, either by upsampling to a higher resolution or downsampling to a lower one. When resampling, it is common to use aggregation methods such as mean, sum, or last value to summarize the data within each time bin. For missing time periods, techniques such as forward fill, backward fill, or interpolation can be employed to estimate values based on the surrounding data. These imputations must be chosen carefully, as inappropriate methods can introduce bias or distort temporal dynamics.

Dealing with missing values in time series is especially delicate. Since the values are not independent, a missing data point represents a break in the sequence, potentially affecting lagged variables, rolling statistics, or model inputs. Forward filling is a common choice, where a missing value is replaced by the most recent previous value. This method assumes that the value remains constant until it is updated, which may be reasonable for certain applications, such as inventory levels. Interpolation, either linear or based on more complex models, can also be effective in estimating missing values while preserving trends. In some contexts, it may be more appropriate to flag missing values with an indicator variable and let the model learn from the missingness pattern itself.

Time-based features are an important component of time series preparation. While raw timestamps are not directly usable by most models, they contain rich information that can be extracted through feature engineering. Deriving attributes such as hour of the day, day of the week, month, quarter, or year helps the model detect seasonality and cyclic patterns. Binary flags for weekends, holidays, or special events can further enhance model awareness of contextual shifts. These features are especially useful in retail, finance, and energy domains, where consumer behavior and market activity follow regular calendars. In some cases, cyclical features should be transformed using sine and cosine functions to preserve their periodic nature and ensure that models do not misinterpret the transition from December to January as a large jump.

Lag features are central to time series modeling, as they allow models to incorporate past information to predict future values. Creating lag features involves shifting the time series by one or more steps, so that each row contains past observations as predictors. The choice of lag values depends on the nature of the data and the domain knowledge about relevant temporal dependencies. Rolling features, such as moving averages or standard deviations, help smooth out noise and capture local trends or volatility. These features are particularly useful in financial forecasting, where short-term momentum or risk indicators are valuable predictors. Exponentially weighted moving averages offer an alternative that gives more weight to recent observations while retaining long-term context.

Another aspect of time series preparation is data splitting. Unlike random sampling used in traditional datasets, time series data must be split in a way that preserves temporal order. Typically, the training set contains earlier observations, and the validation or test set contains later ones. This setup mirrors real-world forecasting scenarios, where future data is unknown and models must be trained on past information. Techniques such as expanding window or sliding window cross-validation allow for robust evaluation by training on incrementally larger subsets and testing on subsequent periods. These approaches ensure that models are not trained on information from the future, which would lead to data leakage and artificially inflated performance.

Detrending and deseasonalizing are additional preprocessing techniques used to stabilize the time series and make it more amenable to modeling. A time series may contain trends, which are long-term increases or decreases in the level of the series, and seasonality, which are recurring patterns tied to calendar cycles. Detrending involves removing the trend component, either by differencing or by subtracting a fitted trend line. Deseasonalizing can be done by calculating seasonal averages and adjusting the data accordingly. These transformations are particularly useful when using models that assume stationarity, where the statistical properties of the series are constant over time. Stationarity is a common assumption in many time series algorithms, such as ARIMA, and ensuring it through proper preparation improves model reliability.

Normalization and scaling also play a role in time series preparation, especially when working with multivariate data or deep learning models. Scaling methods like min-max normalization or standardization help bring all features onto a common scale, which is important for convergence and stability during training. However, scaling must be done with care to prevent data leakage. Statistics used for scaling, such as means and standard deviations, should be calculated only on the training set and then applied to the validation or test sets. This ensures that future information is not inadvertently introduced into the model during preprocessing.

Preparing time series data is a nuanced process that requires a deep understanding of both the data and the temporal context in which it was generated. Each step, from timestamp parsing and resampling to feature engineering and data splitting, plays a crucial role in preserving the sequential nature of the data while making it suitable for analysis. By thoughtfully addressing the unique challenges of time series data, data scientists can build models that capture trends, detect anomalies, and generate accurate forecasts, turning temporal data into a powerful tool for decision-making and strategic insight.

Text Data and Natural Language Basics

Text data is one of the most abundant and valuable forms of information available in the digital world. From emails, news articles, and social media posts to customer reviews, legal documents, and transcripts, text surrounds nearly every industry and discipline. Unlike structured numerical data, however, raw text is unstructured and inherently complex. It does not follow a tabular format and often contains noise, ambiguity, and varied grammar. Working with textual data requires a distinct set of techniques collectively known as natural language processing, or NLP. The goal of NLP is to enable machines to understand, interpret, and generate human language in a way that is both meaningful and useful for analysis and automation.

Before diving into complex models and deep learning algorithms, it is essential to understand the foundational steps involved in working with text data. The first step in any text-based pipeline is cleaning and preprocessing the raw input. This involves removing unwanted characters, punctuation, and symbols that do not carry semantic meaning. Lowercasing all text ensures consistency, as many NLP tools are case-sensitive and treat uppercase and lowercase letters as different tokens. Whitespace normalization, which eliminates excessive spaces and tabs, helps standardize the formatting of the text. These simple transformations contribute to a cleaner and more uniform dataset, making it easier to extract meaningful patterns.

Once the text is cleaned, tokenization is typically the next step. Tokenization involves splitting a string of text into individual units called tokens, which are often words or phrases. For example, the sentence "Data science is powerful" might be tokenized into ["Data", "science", "is", "powerful"]. Tokenization lays the groundwork for virtually all NLP tasks because it transforms a continuous stream of characters into discrete elements that can be analyzed and manipulated. There are various strategies for tokenization, including word-level, sentence-level, and even character-level tokenization, depending on the complexity and goals of the analysis. In languages with complex grammatical rules or no spaces between words, such as Chinese or Japanese, tokenization requires more sophisticated approaches based on linguistic knowledge and statistical methods.

After tokenization, many workflows include the removal of stop words. Stop words are common terms such as "and", "the", "of", and "in" that appear frequently in language but carry little meaningful information for most tasks. By removing these terms, the analysis focuses on content words that are more likely to indicate the subject, sentiment, or intent of a text. However, stop word removal should be applied with caution, as some tasks may benefit from retaining them, especially in domains where these words carry syntactic or semantic significance.

Stemming and lemmatization are techniques used to reduce words to their base or root forms. Stemming uses heuristic rules to strip suffixes from words, converting "running", "runs", and "runner" into the root "run". While fast and easy to implement, stemming can be aggressive and sometimes inaccurate. Lemmatization, on the other hand, uses linguistic knowledge and dictionaries to return the canonical form of a word, considering its part of speech. For example, "better" would be lemmatized to "good", which would not happen with stemming. Lemmatization is generally more accurate but computationally heavier. Both methods aim to reduce the dimensionality of the vocabulary and unify word forms that express the same or similar concepts.

Once the text has been cleaned, tokenized, and normalized, the next step is to represent it numerically. This transformation is necessary because machine learning algorithms operate on numerical data. One of the earliest and most widely used methods is the bag-of-words model, which represents text as a vector of word counts. Each unique word in the vocabulary becomes a feature, and each document is encoded based on the frequency of those words. While simple and effective, this approach ignores word order and semantics, treating all terms as independent features.

To address the limitations of the bag-of-words model, term frequency-inverse document frequency, or TF-IDF, was introduced. TF-IDF adjusts the raw frequency of words by how unique they are across all documents. Words that are common within a specific document but rare across the corpus are given more weight, emphasizing their importance. This method retains the simplicity of bag-of-words but enhances its discriminatory power by downweighting generic terms and upweighting informative ones.

Despite the usefulness of these early models, they lack the ability to capture the semantic meaning of words. Word embeddings represent a significant advancement in text representation by mapping words into dense, continuous vector spaces where similar words have similar vector representations. Models like Word2Vec and GloVe learn these embeddings by analyzing word co-occurrence patterns, capturing subtle relationships such as analogies and similarities. For example, the relationship between "king" and "queen" may mirror that between "man" and "woman". These embeddings can be averaged across a document to represent entire sentences or used as inputs to more complex models.

Contextual embeddings, introduced by modern language models like BERT and GPT, go even further by considering the surrounding context of each word. Unlike traditional embeddings, where each word has a single fixed vector, contextual models assign different vectors depending on the word's role in a sentence. For instance, the word "bank" will have different embeddings in "river bank" and "savings bank", resolving ambiguity through context. These models have revolutionized natural language processing by enabling deeper understanding of syntax, semantics, and even pragmatics.

Text data preparation also involves handling challenges like negation, sarcasm, and ambiguity, which can obscure the true meaning of sentences. Techniques such as dependency parsing and named entity recognition help identify grammatical relationships and extract structured information from unstructured text. Sentiment analysis, topic modeling, and text classification are common applications that benefit from these preparatory steps. Preprocessing lays the foundation for robust models that can infer emotion, intent, and thematic content from written language.

Preparing text data for analysis is a meticulous and iterative process that blends linguistic insight with algorithmic precision. Each step, from cleaning and tokenization to embedding and contextualization, contributes to building a representation of language that machines can interpret and learn from. As natural language processing continues to advance, the foundational techniques remain essential for transforming raw text into structured data. Through this preparation, vast repositories of human expression can be analyzed, modeled, and understood, opening up new possibilities for research, automation, and communication across every sector of society.

Working with Geospatial Data

Geospatial data refers to information that has a geographic or spatial component, representing the location, shape, and relationships of features on the earth's surface. It includes coordinates, addresses, regions, and boundaries tied to real-world places. This data can be used to analyze spatial patterns, model movements, visualize maps, and make informed decisions in fields such as urban planning, transportation, environmental science, agriculture, public health, retail, and emergency response. Working with geospatial data in data science involves specialized techniques and tools that go beyond standard data manipulation, as it requires understanding not only the content of the data but also how it relates to physical space.

The first step in working with geospatial data is understanding the types of data formats commonly used to store location-based information. The most basic form is point data, where each observation is represented by a pair of coordinates, typically in latitude and longitude. Points can denote specific objects like a shop, a bus stop, or a sensor. Line data represents linear features such as roads, rivers, or pipelines, while polygon data is used to define areas like city boundaries, land parcels, or protected zones. These geometries form the foundation of vector data, one of the primary types of geospatial data. In contrast, raster data is a grid of cells or pixels, where each cell represents a spatial value such as elevation, temperature, or satellite imagery. Both vector and raster formats are essential in spatial analysis, depending on the nature of the task.

Coordinate reference systems, or CRS, play a central role in geospatial analysis. These systems define how the two-dimensional, projected map in a dataset relates to real places on the earth. The most common global CRS is the WGS 84 system, which uses degrees of latitude and longitude. However, for precise measurements and local projects, projected coordinate systems like UTM are often used because they minimize distortion over smaller areas. Understanding CRS is critical when combining datasets from different sources. Mismatched coordinate systems can result in misaligned or misplaced features, leading to inaccurate conclusions. Tools like GeoPandas and QGIS allow users to convert between different CRS formats and ensure spatial consistency.

Data acquisition is a crucial aspect of working with geospatial data. Sources of spatial data include government agencies, satellite imagery providers, geographic information systems, and APIs such as OpenStreetMap or Google Maps. These sources offer access to detailed geographic layers, including infrastructure, land use, demographic information, and environmental indicators. When pulling geospatial data from APIs, one often uses bounding boxes, coordinate filters, or spatial queries to limit the scope of the data to the region of interest. Spatial joins and filtering techniques are then used to refine the dataset to relevant observations.

Once the data is acquired, cleaning and preparation become necessary steps. Geospatial data often contains noise, missing values, or inaccuracies in coordinates. Duplicate points, invalid polygons, or empty geometries must be handled to maintain analytical integrity. In addition to traditional data cleaning, spatial data requires checking for topological correctness, such as ensuring that polygons do not intersect improperly or that roads connect logically. Spatial indexing can be implemented to improve the efficiency of operations like point-in-polygon queries or nearest neighbor searches. Libraries such as Shapely and Rtree in Python provide these capabilities, allowing for fast spatial computation.

Visualization is one of the most powerful tools in geospatial data analysis. Plotting locations on a map reveals patterns and anomalies that are difficult to detect in tabular formats. Choropleth maps use color gradients to represent data density or intensity over regions, while heatmaps highlight areas with high concentrations of events. Interactive maps, created with libraries like Folium or Mapbox, enable users to zoom, pan, and explore data dynamically. These visualizations are essential in applications like crime mapping, real estate analysis, and traffic monitoring, where spatial patterns guide strategic decisions. When combined with temporal data, geospatial visualizations can also depict changes over time, such as deforestation, population shifts, or disease spread.

Geospatial analysis goes beyond mapping to include spatial statistics and modeling. Techniques like spatial autocorrelation measure the degree to which a variable is clustered or dispersed across space. Moran's I and Getis-Ord Gi* are common metrics used to quantify spatial patterns. Interpolation methods like kriging or inverse distance weighting allow estimation of values at unsampled locations based on nearby observations. These methods are useful in environmental science and meteorology, where data may only be available at specific points. Spatial regression models extend traditional regression by accounting for spatial dependencies, helping to identify spatially varying relationships that standard models might overlook.

Distance calculations are another cornerstone of geospatial work. Whether estimating travel time, determining proximity to services, or identifying clusters, distance plays a key role in spatial reasoning. Haversine distance is often used for calculations on a spherical surface, such as the earth, while Euclidean distance is suitable for flat projections. More complex routing and navigation tasks involve network analysis, where streets or paths are modeled as graphs. Libraries such as NetworkX or OpenRouteService enable route optimization, accessibility analysis, and service area calculations, supporting applications like logistics, emergency planning, and infrastructure design.

Machine learning with geospatial data introduces additional considerations. Spatial features such as coordinates, distance to landmarks, and neighborhood density can be engineered to enhance predictive power. For instance, a housing price model may include features like proximity to parks, schools, or public transit. Spatial clustering algorithms like DBSCAN and HDBSCAN can identify natural groupings in data based on both location and attribute similarity. These methods are particularly effective in identifying patterns in crime incidents, customer behavior, or ecological observations. When combined with satellite imagery or drone data, convolutional neural networks can be applied to recognize land use, detect changes, or classify terrain, opening new frontiers in geospatial machine learning.

Ethical and privacy concerns are critical when working with geospatial data. Location data, particularly when linked to individuals, raises serious questions about surveillance, consent, and data protection. Anonymization and aggregation techniques are essential to safeguard privacy, especially in applications involving mobile devices, health records, or social media check-ins. Transparency about data sources, usage, and limitations builds trust and ensures responsible use of spatial insights. In humanitarian efforts, urban development, or environmental protection, geospatial data can be a powerful force for good, provided it is handled with care and ethical consideration.

Working with geospatial data combines technical expertise, analytical rigor, and spatial awareness. It requires familiarity with specialized formats, coordinate systems, and visualization techniques, as well as a strong grounding in domain-specific knowledge. By integrating location into data analysis, one unlocks a new dimension of understanding that reveals how geography shapes patterns, behaviors, and outcomes. Whether planning smarter cities, responding to natural disasters, or optimizing supply chains, geospatial data provides the context and clarity necessary to make informed, impactful decisions. As tools and data become more accessible, the ability to think spatially is becoming an indispensable skill for data scientists across disciplines.

Introduction to Databases and SQL

Databases are a fundamental component of modern computing systems and play a critical role in data science workflows. They provide a structured and efficient way to store, organize, retrieve, and manage large volumes of data. A database is essentially a collection of data that is organized so that it can be easily accessed and manipulated. The most common type of database used in data science is the relational database, which stores data in tables consisting of rows and columns. Each table represents a specific entity, and each row within a table represents a record or instance of that entity. Columns represent attributes or fields that describe the characteristics of each record. The power of relational databases lies in their ability to manage complex relationships between data points across different tables using keys and indexes.

Structured Query Language, or SQL, is the standard language used to interact with relational databases. It allows users to perform a wide variety of operations, such as querying data, inserting new records, updating existing entries, and deleting records. SQL also supports the creation and modification of database structures, including the definition of tables, relationships, and constraints. SQL is designed to be declarative, meaning that users specify what they want to retrieve rather than how to retrieve it. This abstraction makes SQL accessible to both technical and non-technical users, while still offering enough power and flexibility to perform sophisticated queries and analyses.

One of the most commonly used SQL operations is the SELECT statement, which is used to retrieve data from one or more tables. A basic SELECT query might retrieve all columns from a single table, but more often, queries are customized to return only the relevant data by specifying particular columns and applying filters with the WHERE clause. The WHERE clause allows users to define conditions that rows must meet to be included in the result set. These conditions can involve equality, inequality, comparisons, or pattern matching, and they can be combined using logical operators like AND, OR, and NOT to construct more complex criteria.

In addition to filtering, SQL supports the ability to sort data using the ORDER BY clause. This allows the user to present results in ascending or descending order based on one or more columns. Aggregation functions such as COUNT, SUM, AVG, MIN, and MAX provide ways to summarize data, and when combined with the GROUP BY clause, they allow for grouped calculations across subsets of the data. This is particularly useful for analyzing data by categories or segments, such as calculating the average salary by department or counting the number of sales per region. The HAVING clause can be used to filter the results of grouped data, enabling further refinement of aggregate queries.

Relational databases also support the concept of joins, which are used to combine data from multiple tables based on related columns. There are several types of joins, including INNER JOIN, LEFT JOIN, RIGHT JOIN, and FULL OUTER JOIN, each with different rules for including or excluding unmatched rows. Joins are a powerful tool for constructing comprehensive views of the data, especially in systems where information is normalized across multiple tables to reduce redundancy and improve data integrity. For example, a database may store customer information in one table and order details in another. By performing a join on the customer ID, analysts can retrieve orders along with the corresponding customer details in a single query.

SQL also includes commands for modifying data, such as INSERT INTO for adding new records, UPDATE for changing existing records, and DELETE for removing records. These commands require careful use, especially in production environments, as improper modifications can lead to data loss or inconsistencies. For this reason, SQL databases typically include features like transactions, which allow a sequence of operations to be executed atomically. Transactions ensure that either all operations succeed or none do, preserving data integrity in the event of errors or failures.

Beyond data manipulation, SQL is also used to define and manage the structure of databases through Data Definition Language (DDL) commands. CREATE TABLE is used to define new tables and specify their columns, data types, and constraints. ALTER TABLE allows changes to existing table structures, such as adding or removing columns or modifying data types. DROP TABLE is used to delete tables entirely, along with their data. Constraints like PRIMARY KEY, FOREIGN KEY, UNIQUE, NOT NULL, and CHECK enforce rules on the data and relationships between tables, helping to maintain accuracy and consistency.

Indexes are another important aspect of database performance. An index is a data structure that improves the speed of data retrieval operations at the cost of additional storage and slower write operations. By creating indexes on columns that are frequently used in search conditions or join operations, query performance can be significantly enhanced. However, excessive indexing can lead to unnecessary overhead, so indexes should be applied judiciously based on query patterns and workload requirements.

Relational databases and SQL are not limited to traditional on-premise systems. Cloud-based solutions such as Amazon RDS, Google Cloud SQL, and Microsoft Azure SQL Database provide scalable, managed environments for relational data. These services offer high availability, automated backups, and seamless integration with other cloud tools. In modern data pipelines, SQL often serves as the interface between raw data and analysis, whether through scheduled queries, ETL processes, or direct connections from data visualization tools.

For data scientists, familiarity with SQL is indispensable. It allows for efficient data extraction, transformation, and loading from relational systems into analytical environments. Tools like Jupyter notebooks and RStudio support SQL integration, enabling analysts to combine code and queries in a unified workflow. Furthermore, many big data platforms, such as Apache Hive and Google BigQuery, use SQL-like syntax to interact with distributed data, extending the relevance of SQL beyond traditional databases.

Understanding the basics of databases and SQL equips data professionals with the ability to access and manipulate the most common form of structured data in the world. It provides a foundation for data analysis, business intelligence, and machine learning workflows. Mastery of SQL opens doors to deeper insights, better data management, and more effective collaboration across teams and disciplines. As data continues to grow in complexity and volume, the ability to harness the power of relational databases remains a cornerstone of effective data science practice.

Using Pandas for Data Manipulation

Pandas is one of the most powerful and widely used libraries in the Python data science ecosystem. It provides high-performance, easy-to-use data structures and data analysis tools that make the process of manipulating and analyzing structured data both intuitive and efficient. Built on top of NumPy, Pandas introduces two primary data structures: the Series and the DataFrame. A Series is essentially a one-dimensional array with axis labels, while a DataFrame is a two-dimensional labeled data structure with columns of potentially different types. These structures form the foundation for virtually all data manipulation tasks performed using Pandas.

One of the key advantages of using Pandas is its ability to handle and transform large datasets quickly and effectively. Data manipulation tasks such as filtering, merging, reshaping, and aggregating can be performed with a few lines of code. The process typically begins with importing the data into a DataFrame from a variety of sources such as CSV files, Excel spreadsheets, SQL databases, or JSON APIs. Once the data is loaded, it becomes accessible in a tabular format, allowing for seamless interaction and inspection. The head() and tail() methods are commonly used to view the first or last few rows of a DataFrame, providing a quick glimpse into its structure.

Data exploration often starts with inspecting column names, data types, and missing values. The info() method reveals the schema of the DataFrame, showing how many non-null entries exist in each column and what their data types are. The describe() method generates summary statistics such as mean, standard deviation, min, and max for numerical columns, which helps in understanding the distribution and range of the data. Identifying and addressing missing values is a critical step in the data cleaning process. Pandas offers functions like isnull() and notnull() to detect null values, and fillna() or dropna() to handle them based on the context and desired outcome.

Filtering and selecting data are fundamental operations in data manipulation. Rows in a DataFrame can be filtered using Boolean indexing, where conditions are applied to columns to create a mask that selects specific entries. For example, selecting all rows where a column meets a certain condition is as simple as writing a logical expression within square brackets. Columns can be accessed individually as Series using the dot notation or by passing the column name within brackets. Multiple columns can be selected by providing a list of column names, resulting in a new DataFrame with the specified subset.

Sorting data is another common task, and Pandas provides the sort_values() method to order rows based on one or more columns, either in ascending or descending order. Sorting can reveal patterns or outliers that might not be immediately visible in the raw dataset. Grouping data using the groupby() function allows for powerful aggregation operations. When data is grouped by a specific feature, such as region or product type, it becomes possible to compute aggregate metrics like sum, average, or count for each group. This is essential for summarizing data and identifying trends across different segments.

Merging and joining datasets is a frequent necessity in real-world data science workflows. Pandas supports SQL-like operations through the merge() function, enabling inner, outer, left, and right joins based on common keys. This makes it easy to combine multiple data sources into a cohesive structure for analysis. Concatenation is another method for combining datasets, typically used when appending rows or columns. The concat() function joins DataFrames along a specified axis, while ensuring that index alignment is preserved or adjusted as necessary. These tools allow data scientists to construct comprehensive datasets from disparate inputs, paving the way for richer analysis.

Reshaping and pivoting data are powerful features in Pandas that facilitate reorganization of datasets to match analytical requirements. The pivot() and pivot_table() methods transform data from a long to a wide format, enabling easier comparisons across variables. Conversely, the melt() function unpivots wide-formatted data into a long format, which is often more suitable for certain types of analysis or visualization. These transformations are essential for preparing data for plotting libraries or statistical models that require specific input formats.

Creating new features or modifying existing ones is a common aspect of feature engineering, and Pandas excels at such tasks. New columns can be created by performing arithmetic operations, applying functions, or combining existing columns. The apply() function is particularly useful for applying custom logic to each row or column, while map() and replace() provide convenient ways to transform values within a Series. These tools enable complex transformations with minimal code, supporting the iterative nature of data preparation and model development.

Datetime manipulation is another area where Pandas offers robust functionality. By converting columns to datetime format using to_datetime(), users can easily extract elements such as year, month, day, weekday, or hour. Time-based indexing allows for filtering data by specific time intervals, while resampling methods like resample() aggregate data over specified frequencies such as daily, weekly, or monthly. These capabilities are indispensable for time series analysis, where understanding temporal trends and patterns is critical.

Handling categorical data is also well-supported in Pandas. Columns can be cast to the category data type, which reduces memory usage and allows for more efficient operations. Categorical data can be encoded using one-hot encoding with the get_dummies() function, preparing the data for machine learning models that require numeric input. This seamless transition from raw categories to numeric representations supports a wide range of modeling techniques without requiring external libraries.

The flexibility and depth of the Pandas library make it an indispensable tool in the data scientist's toolkit. It provides a consistent and expressive interface for a broad range of data manipulation tasks, all while integrating smoothly with the rest of the Python data science stack. Whether performing exploratory analysis, cleaning messy data, engineering new features, or preparing inputs for modeling, Pandas offers the tools and performance required to work efficiently and effectively. Mastery of Pandas enables data scientists to tackle real-world problems with confidence, turning raw datasets into structured insights that drive impactful decisions.

Data Visualization with Matplotlib and Seaborn

Data visualization is a central component of data analysis and storytelling. It transforms raw numbers into visual forms that are easier to interpret and explore. In Python, two of the most popular libraries for creating visualizations are Matplotlib and Seaborn. Matplotlib is a foundational library that provides fine-grained control over plot construction and customization. It is extremely flexible, allowing users to create a wide variety of plots, from basic line graphs to complex multi-panel figures. Seaborn is built on top of Matplotlib and is designed to make the process of creating attractive and informative statistical graphics simpler and more intuitive. It comes with built-in themes, color palettes, and functions for visualizing distributions, relationships, and categorical data, making it especially useful for exploratory data analysis.

Working with Matplotlib often begins by importing the pyplot module, which provides a MATLAB-like interface to the plotting functions. The most basic plot is a line chart, created using the plot function with a list or array of values. By default, Matplotlib connects each point with a line, but various markers and line styles can be specified to customize the appearance. Titles, axis labels, legends, and grid lines can all be added using individual function calls. The figure and axes model in Matplotlib offers an object-oriented approach for more complex plots. This model separates the canvas (figure) from the individual plotting areas (axes), which allows for precise control over multiple subplots and layout adjustments.

Seaborn simplifies many common visualization tasks by abstracting some of the lower-level details that Matplotlib requires. For example, a simple histogram or bar plot can be generated in Seaborn with a single function call and minimal setup. Seaborn also integrates seamlessly with Pandas DataFrames, allowing users to pass in data and specify variables by column names. This leads to more readable and concise code. One of the core strengths of Seaborn is its ability to handle statistical visualizations. Functions like distplot, histplot, kdeplot, and boxplot provide immediate insight into data distributions, variability, and outliers. These plots help analysts understand the shape, center, and spread of their data at a glance.

When analyzing relationships between variables, scatter plots and line plots are often the first step. Seaborn's scatterplot and lineplot functions make it easy to plot bivariate relationships, including optional grouping by color or style to distinguish subgroups within the data. For more complex pairwise visualizations, Seaborn offers the pairplot function, which generates a matrix of scatter plots and histograms for multiple variables at once. This is extremely useful when exploring a new dataset and looking for trends or correlations. The heatmap function in Seaborn is another powerful tool that can be used to visualize matrices of data, such as correlation coefficients. It uses color intensity to convey values, allowing for quick identification of strong relationships or anomalies within the dataset.

Categorical variables require different visualization techniques. Seaborn offers specialized functions like barplot, countplot, boxplot, violinplot, and swarmplot, each designed to reveal different aspects of the data. For instance, boxplots display the distribution of a variable across categories, including the median, quartiles, and potential outliers. Violin plots go a step further by adding a kernel density estimate to show the distribution shape within each category. Swarm plots represent individual data points and prevent them from overlapping, giving a clearer view of sample sizes and distributions. These visualizations are particularly valuable in comparing groups and identifying significant differences or patterns.

Styling and customization are important in creating effective visualizations. Both Matplotlib and Seaborn offer a variety of options for adjusting colors, fonts, line widths, and other aesthetic elements. Seaborn includes built-in themes such as darkgrid, whitegrid, and ticks, which can be set globally to maintain consistency across plots. Color palettes can be customized to match branding guidelines or improve accessibility, including colorblind-friendly options. Annotations can be added to highlight specific points, and axis scales can be adjusted to log or categorical formats depending on the nature of the data. These enhancements help make plots not only informative but also visually appealing and easy to interpret.

Subplots and figure layouts allow analysts to present multiple views of the data simultaneously. Matplotlib's subplots function creates a grid of plots that share a figure, making it easier to compare related metrics or display different dimensions of the same dataset. Seaborn plots can be combined in subplots by specifying axes objects or using FacetGrid, a powerful feature that allows for automatic generation of plots across rows and columns based on categorical variables. This is especially useful in examining how distributions or relationships vary across different groups or time periods. The tight_layout function in Matplotlib ensures that plots do not overlap, maintaining readability even in dense figure arrangements.

Interactive visualization is another growing area, and while Matplotlib and Seaborn are primarily static plotting libraries, they can be used in conjunction with tools like Jupyter notebooks to create dynamic visualizations. By integrating widgets and using libraries such as ipywidgets or Plotly, analysts can allow users to explore different facets of the data by adjusting parameters on the fly. Although this adds complexity, it greatly enhances user engagement and understanding, especially in presentations or reports shared with non-technical stakeholders.

Saving and exporting plots is often the final step in the visualization process. Both Matplotlib and Seaborn support saving figures in various formats including PNG, PDF, SVG, and EPS. The savefig function allows users to specify resolution, figure size, and file format, making it easy to generate publication-quality graphics. Exported plots can be embedded in reports, dashboards, or presentations, ensuring that insights derived from analysis can be communicated effectively and persuasively to broader audiences.

Learning to visualize data effectively with Matplotlib and Seaborn is not only about mastering functions and syntax but also about developing an analytical mindset that seeks clarity, precision, and insight. Good visualization communicates data-driven stories in a way that numerical tables alone cannot. It reveals structure, highlights variation, and supports hypotheses through visual evidence. Whether analyzing trends, comparing categories, or exploring correlations, the combination of Matplotlib's flexibility and Seaborn's elegance makes them indispensable tools in the data science workflow. Through consistent practice and thoughtful design, these libraries empower data scientists to transform raw data into compelling visual narratives that drive understanding, discovery, and action.

Introduction to Machine Learning

Machine learning is a subfield of artificial intelligence that focuses on developing algorithms that allow computers to learn from and make decisions or predictions based on data. Unlike traditional programming, where explicit instructions are provided for every task, machine learning enables systems to identify patterns, extract insights, and improve their performance over time without being explicitly programmed for each possible scenario. At its core, machine learning involves feeding large amounts of data into algorithms that can generalize from examples and make intelligent predictions or decisions when faced with new, unseen data.

The process of machine learning typically begins with a well-defined problem and a dataset that contains examples relevant to that problem. These examples usually consist of input features, which describe the characteristics of each observation, and output labels or targets, which represent the outcome or class that the model is trying to predict. The model learns to map inputs to outputs by identifying relationships and patterns in the training data. Once trained, the model can be applied to new data to generate predictions, classify observations, or detect anomalies. The quality and quantity of the data are critical to the success of machine learning. Clean, diverse, and representative data leads to better generalization and more reliable predictions.

There are several types of machine learning, each suited to different kinds of tasks. The two primary categories are supervised and unsupervised learning. In supervised learning, the training data includes both input features and known output labels. The goal is for the algorithm to learn the mapping function from inputs to outputs so it can accurately predict the output for new inputs. Common supervised learning tasks include classification, where the goal is to assign each input to a predefined category, and regression, where the goal is to predict a continuous numeric value. Examples include spam detection, disease diagnosis, credit scoring, and price forecasting.

Unsupervised learning, by contrast, deals with data that does not have labeled outputs. The algorithm tries to uncover hidden patterns or structures in the data without guidance on what the output should be. Clustering and dimensionality reduction are typical unsupervised learning tasks. Clustering involves grouping similar observations together based on their features, while dimensionality reduction aims to simplify datasets by reducing the number of variables while preserving as much information as possible. Applications include customer segmentation, anomaly detection, and visualization of high-dimensional data.

There is also a growing area of machine learning known as reinforcement learning, in which an agent learns to make decisions by interacting with an environment. The agent receives feedback in the form of rewards or penalties based on its actions and seeks to maximize cumulative rewards over time. Reinforcement learning has been successfully applied in robotics, game playing, and recommendation systems, and it represents a blend of decision-making, learning, and optimization.

The machine learning workflow involves several key steps. First, the data must be collected, cleaned, and preprocessed. This includes handling missing values, encoding categorical variables, scaling numerical features, and splitting the dataset into training and test subsets. Feature engineering may be performed to extract or create new variables that better represent the underlying patterns in the data. Once the data is ready, a suitable algorithm is chosen based on the problem type, data characteristics, and performance requirements.

Model training involves fitting the chosen algorithm to the training data. During this process, the model adjusts its internal parameters to minimize the error between its predictions and the actual target values. The optimization is typically done using techniques such as gradient descent, which iteratively updates the model parameters to reduce a loss function. The loss function quantifies the discrepancy between predicted and actual values and guides the learning process. For example, in regression problems, mean squared error is often used as the loss function, while classification problems may use cross-entropy loss or hinge loss.

After training, the model is evaluated using the test set or through cross-validation. Performance metrics depend on the type of task. For classification, accuracy, precision, recall, F1-score, and the area under the ROC curve are commonly used. For regression, metrics such as mean absolute error, mean squared error, and R-squared are typical. These metrics help assess how well the model is performing and whether it is generalizing well to new data. If the model performs poorly, adjustments can be made by tuning hyperparameters, selecting different features, or trying alternative algorithms.

Popular machine learning algorithms include linear regression, logistic regression, decision trees, random forests, support vector machines, k-nearest neighbors, and naive Bayes. More advanced methods include ensemble techniques like gradient boosting, as well as neural networks, which are especially powerful for tasks involving images, text, or complex patterns. Choosing the right algorithm depends on the problem context, the size and type of data, and the interpretability and speed requirements of the application.

Overfitting and underfitting are common challenges in machine learning. Overfitting occurs when a model learns the noise or random fluctuations in the training data rather than the true underlying patterns. This leads to excellent performance on the training data but poor generalization to new data. Underfitting happens when the model is too simple to capture the complexity of the data, resulting in poor performance on both the training and test data. Techniques such as regularization, cross-validation, and early stopping are used to address these issues and improve model robustness.

Model deployment is the final step in the machine learning pipeline. Once a model is trained and validated, it must be integrated into a real-world system to make predictions on live data. This involves building APIs, creating user interfaces, and ensuring that the model continues to perform well over time. Monitoring the model in production is essential, as data distributions may shift, leading to degradation in performance. Retraining the model with new data and updating it regularly is part of the maintenance process in real-world machine learning systems.

Machine learning is transforming industries and reshaping the way decisions are made across sectors. From predicting customer behavior to detecting fraud, from diagnosing diseases to personalizing recommendations, machine learning offers a powerful toolkit for turning data into actionable insights. It is a field that combines statistical rigor, computational power, and human intuition, and it continues to evolve rapidly with advances in algorithms, computing, and data availability. As the world becomes increasingly data-driven, understanding the foundations of machine learning is essential for anyone seeking to leverage data in innovative and impactful ways.

Supervised vs Unsupervised Learning

In the field of machine learning, one of the most fundamental distinctions is between supervised and unsupervised learning. These two paradigms represent different approaches to training algorithms, each suited to different types of problems and data structures. Understanding the differences between them is essential for selecting the right techniques, designing effective workflows, and ultimately extracting meaningful insights from data. Both supervised and unsupervised learning rely on the core idea that machines can learn patterns from data, but they do so under very different assumptions and with distinct types of guidance.

Supervised learning is defined by the presence of labeled data. This means that each training example in the dataset includes both input features and an associated output label or target. The goal of supervised learning is to learn a function that maps inputs to outputs by observing many such input-output pairs. During training, the algorithm adjusts its internal parameters to minimize the difference between the predicted outputs and the actual labels. Once the model is trained, it can be used to make predictions on new, unseen data by applying the learned mapping. Supervised learning is particularly powerful for predictive tasks where historical examples can guide future decisions.

There are two primary types of supervised learning tasks: classification and regression. In classification problems, the output label represents a category or class, and the model's task is to assign each input to one of those predefined classes. Examples include detecting spam emails, identifying handwritten digits, or diagnosing medical conditions based on patient data. In regression problems, the output label is a continuous numeric value, and the model predicts a real number based on the input features. Common regression applications include predicting house prices, forecasting sales, or estimating insurance costs. In both cases, performance is evaluated by comparing the model's predictions to the true labels using appropriate metrics such as accuracy, precision, recall, mean squared error, or R-squared.

Supervised learning benefits from clear objectives and measurable outcomes, making it suitable for tasks where the ground truth is available. However, it relies heavily on the availability and quality of labeled data. In many real-world scenarios, obtaining labeled data can be expensive, time-consuming, or impractical. For example, labeling images for object recognition or transcribing hours of speech for voice recognition requires human expertise and effort. Moreover, supervised models can be sensitive to biases present in the training data, and if not carefully curated, they may perpetuate or amplify these biases in their predictions.

Unsupervised learning, by contrast, deals with data that does not include output labels. The objective is to discover hidden structures, patterns, or groupings within the data without explicit guidance. Rather than predicting an outcome, unsupervised learning seeks to explore the data, summarize its structure, or reduce its complexity. It is often used for exploratory data analysis, dimensionality reduction, and clustering. The absence of labels makes unsupervised learning more flexible and broadly applicable, especially in situations where labels are unavailable or unknown.

Clustering is one of the most common tasks in unsupervised learning. It involves partitioning a dataset into distinct groups or clusters such that data points within the same cluster are more similar to each other than to those in other clusters. Algorithms like k-means, hierarchical clustering, and DBSCAN are widely used to perform clustering. These methods help identify natural groupings in data, such as customer segments, document topics, or genetic populations. Clustering is particularly valuable in market research, social network analysis, and image segmentation.

Another important unsupervised learning technique is dimensionality reduction, which involves transforming high-dimensional data into a lower-dimensional space while preserving its essential structure. Techniques like principal component analysis and t-distributed stochastic neighbor embedding are commonly used for this purpose. Dimensionality reduction is useful for visualizing complex data, reducing noise, and improving the performance of other machine learning models. It can reveal latent variables, simplify modeling tasks, and highlight the most informative features in the data.

Unsupervised learning presents its own challenges. Since there are no labels, it is difficult to evaluate model performance using standard metrics. Interpretation of results often relies on domain knowledge and visual inspection. For example, in clustering, determining the optimal number of clusters is not always straightforward and may require trial and error or the use of statistical validation techniques like the silhouette score or the elbow method. Moreover, unsupervised algorithms can sometimes identify patterns that are mathematically significant but not meaningful in a real-world context. This makes validation and interpretation especially critical.

Despite their differences, supervised and unsupervised learning are not mutually exclusive. In practice, they often complement each other. Unsupervised learning can be used as a preprocessing step for supervised tasks, helping to reduce dimensionality, detect outliers, or identify features that are most predictive. It can also help in understanding the structure of the data before applying supervised methods. On the other hand, semi-supervised learning and self-supervised learning represent hybrid approaches that leverage both labeled and unlabeled data to improve learning efficiency and performance. These methods are gaining traction in areas like computer vision and natural language processing, where vast amounts of data are available but only a small fraction is labeled.

The choice between supervised and unsupervised learning depends on several factors, including the availability of labeled data, the goals of the analysis, and the nature of the problem. Supervised learning is ideal for tasks that require accurate prediction or classification and where sufficient labeled data exists. Unsupervised learning is better suited for exploratory analysis, pattern discovery, and scenarios where the data lacks predefined categories or labels. Mastering both approaches allows data scientists to handle a wide range of analytical challenges, adapt to various data environments, and develop more comprehensive solutions.

Understanding the distinction between supervised and unsupervised learning provides a foundational framework for approaching machine learning problems. It shapes how data is prepared, how algorithms are selected, and how results are interpreted. As machine learning continues to evolve, the ability to navigate and integrate both supervised and unsupervised methods becomes increasingly important. These two learning paradigms represent not only different technical strategies but also different ways of thinking about data, discovery, and the role of algorithms in extracting value from information.

Building Regression Models

Regression models are among the most fundamental and widely used tools in the field of machine learning and statistics. They are designed to model the relationship between a dependent variable, often referred to as the target or outcome, and one or more independent variables, known as features or predictors. The main goal of regression is to predict continuous outcomes by learning from existing data. Building a regression model involves several key steps, including understanding the problem, preparing the data, selecting the appropriate model, training it, evaluating its performance, and interpreting the results. Each step plays a crucial role in ensuring the model is both accurate and generalizable.

The process of building a regression model starts with understanding the context and the nature of the problem at hand. It is essential to determine whether the outcome variable is continuous and whether the relationships between the variables are likely to be linear or nonlinear. This understanding informs the choice of model and the techniques used throughout the modeling process. For instance, predicting house prices, sales revenue, or temperature readings are typical regression tasks where the target variable is a real number that varies across a range.

Once the problem is clearly defined, the next step is data preparation. This involves collecting and cleaning the dataset, handling missing values, encoding categorical variables, and performing feature scaling if necessary. Data quality is paramount because the performance of any regression model is directly tied to the quality of the input data. Irrelevant or noisy features can lead to poor model accuracy, while missing or inconsistent values can cause training failures or biased predictions. Exploratory data analysis helps identify patterns, outliers, and correlations among variables, all of which can guide feature selection and transformation.

With clean and well-understood data, the next step is to choose a suitable regression algorithm. The simplest and most interpretable regression model is linear regression. In linear regression, the relationship between the target and predictors is assumed to be linear, meaning the change in the target is proportional to the change in the predictors. The model fits a straight line to the data by minimizing the difference between the observed values and the predicted values, often using a method called ordinary least squares. This method finds the coefficients that minimize the sum of squared residuals, which are the differences between the actual and predicted values.

For more complex relationships, other regression techniques may be more appropriate. Polynomial regression can model curved relationships by adding higher-degree terms to the model. Ridge and Lasso regression are regularized versions of linear regression that include penalties for large coefficients, helping to prevent overfitting, especially in cases with many correlated features. Ridge regression penalizes the sum of squared coefficients, while Lasso regression penalizes the sum of the absolute values, often leading to sparse models where some coefficients are exactly zero. Elastic Net combines both penalties and can be a useful compromise when dealing with high-dimensional data.

Another popular technique is decision tree regression, which divides the data into regions based on feature values and predicts the outcome using the average value in each region. Random forest regression, an ensemble method based on decision trees, builds multiple trees on different subsets of the data and averages their predictions, improving accuracy and robustness. Gradient boosting regression further improves performance by sequentially building trees that correct the errors of previous ones. These advanced models can capture complex nonlinear relationships and interactions between features that linear models may miss.

After selecting and training a regression model, it is essential to evaluate its performance. The dataset is typically split into training and test sets to assess how well the model generalizes to unseen data.

Performance metrics for regression include mean absolute error, mean squared error, root mean squared error, and the coefficient of determination, commonly known as R-squared. Mean absolute error measures the average magnitude of the errors without considering their direction. Mean squared error penalizes larger errors more heavily by squaring the residuals. Root mean squared error is the square root of mean squared error and is often used because it has the same units as the target variable. R-squared indicates the proportion of variance in the target variable that is explained by the predictors and ranges from zero to one, with higher values indicating better performance.

Residual analysis is another crucial part of regression modeling. By plotting the residuals, which are the differences between observed and predicted values, analysts can check for patterns that indicate problems such as nonlinearity, heteroscedasticity, or autocorrelation. Ideally, residuals should be randomly distributed with constant variance. Any visible structure suggests that the model is missing key relationships or assumptions are being violated. In such cases, additional features, transformations, or alternative models may be needed.

Feature importance and interpretability are also important considerations in regression modeling. In linear regression, the coefficients directly indicate the impact of each predictor on the target variable, assuming all other variables are held constant. Positive coefficients suggest a direct relationship, while negative coefficients indicate an inverse relationship. Standardized coefficients, where features are scaled to have mean zero and unit variance, can be used to compare the relative importance of different predictors. In tree-based models, feature importance can be assessed by examining how much each feature contributes to reducing error in the splits. This information helps identify which variables are most influential in making predictions.

Deploying a regression model involves integrating it into a real-world system where it can generate predictions on new data. This step includes saving the trained model, creating interfaces for input and output, and ensuring that the model continues to perform well over time. Monitoring is critical because data distributions can change, leading to model drift and reduced accuracy. Periodic retraining with updated data helps maintain model relevance and reliability.

Building regression models is a process that blends statistical rigor, domain expertise, and practical considerations. It requires not only technical skill in selecting and tuning algorithms but also a deep understanding of the problem context and the data. Whether using simple linear models for quick insights or complex ensemble methods for high accuracy, the goal remains the same: to capture the underlying patterns in data and use them to make informed, actionable predictions. Through careful preparation, thoughtful modeling, and continuous evaluation, regression models become powerful tools for turning data into knowledge.

Classification Algorithms in Practice

Classification is one of the most common and essential tasks in machine learning, focused on assigning input data to predefined categories or classes. Unlike regression, where the goal is to predict continuous values, classification deals with discrete outputs. Practical applications of classification algorithms are found in nearly every industry and include tasks such as spam detection, sentiment analysis, medical diagnosis, fraud detection, image recognition, and customer churn prediction. Building and applying classification algorithms in practice requires a clear understanding of the problem domain, data preparation, model selection, training, evaluation, and deployment.

The process begins with a dataset that includes labeled examples. Each observation in the dataset consists of input features and a corresponding class label. These class labels may represent binary outcomes such as positive or negative, or they may represent multiple classes, such as types of animals, customer segments, or product categories. A well-constructed classification model learns from these examples and is able to generalize the mapping from input features to labels so that it can correctly classify new, unseen observations.

One of the simplest and most interpretable classification algorithms is logistic regression. Despite its name, logistic regression is used for classification tasks, particularly binary classification. It models the probability that an observation belongs to a particular class using the logistic function, which outputs values between zero and one. The predicted probability is then thresholded, typically at 0.5, to assign a class label. Logistic regression assumes a linear relationship between the features and the log-odds of the outcome. It is easy to implement and interpret, making it a common starting point for binary classification problems.

Another widely used algorithm is the k-nearest neighbors classifier. This non-parametric method classifies an observation based on the majority class of its k closest neighbors in the feature space. The algorithm relies on a distance metric, such as Euclidean distance, to determine proximity between points. K-nearest neighbors is simple and effective for datasets with clearly defined boundaries between classes, but it can be computationally expensive for large datasets and sensitive to irrelevant or redundant features. Choosing the optimal value of k and applying feature scaling are important steps in using this method effectively.

Decision trees offer a more flexible and interpretable approach to classification. A decision tree splits the dataset into subsets based on feature values, forming a tree-like structure where each node represents a decision point. The leaves of the tree correspond to class labels. Decision trees handle both numerical and categorical features and can capture complex interactions between variables. They are easy to visualize and understand, but they can be prone to overfitting if not pruned or regularized. Random forests address this issue by building an ensemble of decision trees using bootstrapped samples and averaging their predictions. This reduces variance and improves generalization, making random forests one of the most powerful and reliable classification methods in practice.

Support vector machines are another effective classification algorithm, particularly when the data is high-dimensional or not linearly separable. A support vector machine constructs a hyperplane that maximally separates the classes in the feature space. The algorithm seeks the decision boundary that provides the largest margin between the classes, defined by the support vectors, which are the data points closest to the boundary. For nonlinear problems, the kernel trick allows support vector machines to project the data into a higher-dimensional space where it becomes linearly separable. This flexibility makes SVMs highly effective, but they can be computationally intensive and sensitive to the choice of kernel and hyperparameters.

Naive Bayes classifiers are based on Bayes' theorem and assume that features are conditionally independent given the class label. Despite this strong and often unrealistic assumption, naive Bayes performs surprisingly well in many applications, particularly in text classification and spam detection. It is fast, requires little training data, and provides probabilistic predictions that can be useful in decision-making processes. The algorithm is particularly effective when working with high-dimensional data, where other models may struggle due to the curse of dimensionality.

In recent years, gradient boosting machines have gained popularity for their accuracy and robustness in a wide range of classification tasks. Algorithms such as XGBoost, LightGBM, and CatBoost build an ensemble of weak learners, typically decision trees, in a sequential manner. Each new tree is trained to correct the errors of the previous ones, and the final model is a weighted sum of all the trees. Gradient boosting is highly effective at capturing complex patterns and handling different types of data, but it requires careful tuning and can be prone to overfitting if not properly regularized.

Evaluating classification models involves more than just measuring overall accuracy. Depending on the application, metrics such as precision, recall, F1-score, and the area under the ROC curve may provide more insight into model performance. Accuracy can be misleading in cases where class imbalance exists. For example, in fraud detection, the number of fraudulent transactions may be very small compared to legitimate ones. In such cases, a model that predicts all transactions as legitimate would have high accuracy but be useless in practice. Precision measures the proportion of true positives among predicted positives, while recall measures the proportion of true positives among actual positives. The F1-score is the harmonic mean of precision and recall, providing a balanced measure that is especially useful when the cost of false positives and false negatives differs.

In practical applications, the choice of classification algorithm depends on several factors, including the size and dimensionality of the data, the presence of missing or noisy values, the interpretability requirements, and the computational resources available. Model selection often involves experimentation with multiple algorithms, feature sets, and hyperparameters. Cross-validation helps ensure that performance metrics are reliable and that the model generalizes well to new data.

Once a model is trained and validated, it can be deployed into production environments where it makes real-time or batch predictions. This involves saving the model, integrating it into an application or pipeline, and continuously monitoring its performance. Data drift, where the distribution of input data changes over time, can degrade model accuracy and necessitate retraining or adaptation. Maintaining classification models in production requires regular evaluation, updates, and collaboration between data scientists, engineers, and domain experts.

Classification algorithms are powerful tools that convert raw data into actionable decisions. They enable organizations to automate processes, detect risks, personalize experiences, and uncover hidden insights. While building effective classifiers involves careful data preparation, thoughtful model selection, and rigorous evaluation, the potential benefits are significant. As machine learning continues to evolve, the practical application of classification algorithms will remain at the heart of intelligent systems and data-driven innovation.

Model Evaluation Metrics

Evaluating machine learning models is a critical step in the data science pipeline. A model's ability to make accurate predictions, generalize to unseen data, and perform consistently in real-world scenarios depends heavily on how it is assessed. Model evaluation metrics provide the quantitative tools needed to measure a model's performance and guide the decision-making process during model development. The choice of evaluation metric is not universal; it depends on the type of problem being solved, whether it is a classification or regression task, the nature of the data, and the specific business or research objectives behind the analysis. Selecting the right metrics is essential for developing robust models and avoiding misleading conclusions.

For classification problems, where the goal is to assign input instances to predefined categories, accuracy is one of the most straightforward and widely used metrics. Accuracy is calculated as the ratio of correctly predicted observations to the total number of observations. While easy to interpret, accuracy can be deceptive, especially when dealing with imbalanced datasets where one class significantly outnumbers the others. In such cases, a model might achieve high accuracy by simply predicting the majority class, even if it fails completely to identify the minority class. This limitation highlights the need for alternative metrics that provide a more nuanced view of model performance.

Precision and recall are two metrics that address the shortcomings of accuracy in imbalanced classification tasks. Precision measures the proportion of true positive predictions among all instances predicted as positive. High precision indicates that the model does not generate many false positives, which is important in contexts where incorrect positive predictions are costly, such as fraud detection or medical diagnosis. Recall, on the other hand, measures the proportion of true positive instances that were correctly identified by the model. A high recall means the model is able to detect most of the relevant cases, which is crucial when missing a positive instance is more detrimental than making a false alarm. The trade-off between precision and recall is often visualized using a precision-recall curve, which helps in understanding how the model behaves under different classification thresholds.

To balance precision and recall, the F_1-score is used as a single metric that combines both. The F_1-score is the harmonic mean of precision and recall, giving equal weight to both metrics. It is particularly useful when a balance between false positives and false negatives is desired. In multiclass classification tasks, F_1-scores can be computed for each class and then averaged using macro, micro, or weighted methods depending on the specific evaluation needs. These approaches allow practitioners to account for class imbalance and ensure that performance is measured comprehensively across all categories.

Another powerful tool for classification evaluation is the confusion matrix, which provides a tabular summary of prediction outcomes. It breaks down predictions into true positives, true negatives, false positives, and false negatives, allowing for a more granular analysis of errors. By examining the confusion matrix, one can identify systematic biases, such as a tendency to misclassify certain classes, and adjust the model or data accordingly. The confusion matrix serves as a foundation for many derived metrics and is an indispensable diagnostic tool in classification analysis.

For binary classification, the Receiver Operating Characteristic curve, or ROC curve, is commonly used to evaluate model performance across different threshold settings. The ROC curve plots the true positive rate against the false positive rate and illustrates the trade-off between sensitivity and specificity. The area under the ROC curve, or AUC, is a single scalar value that summarizes the overall ability of the model to distinguish between classes. A model with an AUC close to one has excellent discriminative ability, while an AUC close to 0.5 indicates no better performance than random guessing. AUC-ROC is particularly useful when the cost of false positives and false negatives is unknown or variable.

In regression tasks, where the goal is to predict continuous values, different metrics are required. One of the most commonly used regression metrics is Mean Absolute Error, or MAE. It measures the average magnitude of the errors in predictions, without considering their direction. MAE is intuitive and interpretable, making it useful when all errors are equally significant. Mean Squared Error, or MSE, takes a different approach by squaring the errors before averaging them, thereby penalizing larger errors more heavily. This makes MSE more sensitive to outliers, which can be beneficial or problematic depending on the context. Root Mean Squared Error, or RMSE, is the square root of MSE and has the same units as the target variable, making it easier to interpret in the context of the original data.

Another important regression metric is R-squared, or the coefficient of determination. R-squared measures the proportion of variance in the dependent variable that is predictable from the independent variables. It ranges from zero to one, with higher values indicating a better fit. However, R-squared alone does not tell the full story. It can be inflated by adding irrelevant features to the model, so it is often complemented by Adjusted R-squared, which penalizes the addition of features that do not improve the model's explanatory power. In some cases, especially when evaluating model generalization, metrics such as Mean Absolute Percentage Error (MAPE) or Median Absolute Error are used to provide additional perspectives on performance.

Model evaluation also includes considerations of cross-validation, which helps estimate how well a model will perform on unseen data. Instead of relying on a single train-test split, k-fold cross-validation divides the data into multiple subsets and rotates the training and testing roles, reducing the variability of the evaluation. This approach provides a more robust estimate of model performance and helps detect overfitting or underfitting. Evaluating models with multiple metrics across cross-validation folds gives a more comprehensive understanding of how a model behaves under different data conditions.

Beyond numeric metrics, interpretability and explainability are increasingly recognized as essential components of model evaluation, particularly in high-stakes domains such as healthcare, finance, and law. Tools like SHAP values and LIME allow practitioners to assess how individual features contribute to predictions, improving transparency and trust in the model. Evaluating models is not just about performance numbers but also about understanding behavior, identifying biases, and ensuring ethical and fair outcomes.

The process of model evaluation is iterative and dynamic. As new data becomes available or as the modeling goals evolve, the chosen metrics may need to be revisited and updated. Model performance should be monitored over time to detect drift or degradation, prompting retraining or recalibration when necessary. Effective evaluation is the backbone of successful machine learning projects, guiding every step from model selection to deployment and maintenance. A deep understanding of evaluation metrics empowers data scientists to build models that are not only accurate but also reliable, interpretable, and aligned with the objectives they are designed to serve.

Decision Trees and Random Forests

Decision trees and random forests are among the most popular and powerful machine learning algorithms used for both classification and regression tasks. Their popularity stems from their intuitive structure, ease of interpretation, and strong performance across a wide range of datasets. These algorithms model data using a tree-like structure where decisions are made at each node based on the value of input features, leading to predictions at the leaf nodes. While decision trees offer simplicity and transparency, random forests enhance predictive accuracy and robustness by combining the strengths of many individual decision trees into an ensemble.

A decision tree is built by recursively partitioning the data into subsets based on feature values that maximize some metric of purity, such as information gain, Gini impurity, or variance reduction. The algorithm begins at the root node with the entire dataset and selects the feature and threshold that best separates the data according to the chosen criterion. This process is repeated for each resulting subset, creating child nodes, until a stopping condition is met. Stopping conditions can include a maximum depth, a minimum number of samples per leaf, or a minimum impurity decrease. The final model consists of a hierarchy of decision rules that can be easily followed to arrive at a prediction.

In classification tasks, decision trees aim to create nodes that are as pure as possible, meaning that most of the observations in a node belong to the same class. The Gini impurity is commonly used to measure this purity, quantifying how often a randomly chosen element from the set would be incorrectly labeled. Information gain, based on entropy, is another criterion that evaluates the reduction in uncertainty achieved by a split. In regression tasks, the goal is to minimize the variance of the target variable within each node. The splitting criterion in this case is typically the reduction in mean squared error.

One of the most appealing aspects of decision trees is their interpretability. The structure of the tree can be visualized and understood by non-technical stakeholders, making it easy to explain how decisions are made. Each path from the root to a leaf represents a decision rule that classifies or predicts outcomes. This transparency makes decision trees attractive in fields such as finance, healthcare, and legal analytics, where model interpretability is critical for trust and accountability.

However, decision trees have several limitations. They are prone to overfitting, especially when allowed to grow deep and complex. A deep tree can capture noise and idiosyncrasies in the training data, leading to poor generalization to new data. Pruning techniques can be applied to simplify the tree by removing branches that have little impact on the final prediction. Pre-pruning, which involves setting limits during the growth process, and post-pruning, which trims the tree after it has fully grown, are both used to control complexity and reduce overfitting.

To overcome the limitations of a single decision tree, random forests employ an ensemble approach. A random forest builds multiple decision trees and aggregates their predictions to produce a final result. For classification, the forest takes a majority vote across the trees, and for regression, it averages the predictions. This ensemble method improves accuracy, reduces variance, and enhances robustness. The key to the effectiveness of random forests lies in the diversity of the individual trees. To encourage diversity, each tree is trained on a different bootstrap sample of the data, and at each split, only a random subset of features is considered. This randomness reduces correlation between trees and prevents them from all converging on the same model.

Random forests offer several advantages over single decision trees. They are less likely to overfit, especially when the number of trees is large. They handle large datasets and high-dimensional feature spaces well. They are capable of modeling complex nonlinear relationships and interactions between features. Additionally, random forests provide estimates of feature importance, which can help identify which variables are most influential in the prediction. This information can be used for feature selection, model interpretation, and gaining insights into the underlying data patterns.

Training a random forest involves several hyperparameters that can be tuned to optimize performance. These include the number of trees in the forest, the maximum depth of each tree, the minimum number of samples required to split a node, and the number of features to consider at each split. Grid search and cross-validation are commonly used to find the best combination of hyperparameters. Although random forests are computationally more intensive than single decision trees, modern implementations and parallel processing capabilities make them scalable and efficient even for large-scale problems.

Despite their many strengths, random forests also have limitations. While they provide better accuracy than individual trees, they sacrifice interpretability. The ensemble nature of the model means that it is not straightforward to trace how a particular prediction was made, making it less transparent than a single decision tree. Tools such as partial dependence plots and tree interpreters can help in understanding the behavior of the model, but they do not offer the same simplicity as a single path through a tree.

Random forests are also less effective when the data contains a large number of irrelevant features or when the target variable depends on a small number of features in a complex way. In such cases, more specialized algorithms like gradient boosting may outperform random forests. Nonetheless, random forests remain a go-to algorithm in many practical scenarios due to their versatility, reliability, and strong out-of-the-box performance.

In practice, decision trees and random forests are widely used in real-world applications across various domains. In finance, they are employed for credit scoring, risk assessment, and algorithmic trading. In healthcare, they assist in disease diagnosis, patient segmentation, and treatment recommendations. In e-commerce, they power recommendation systems, customer segmentation, and fraud detection. Their ability to handle both numerical and categorical data, deal with missing values, and scale to large datasets makes them indispensable tools in the data scientist's toolkit.

Building and deploying decision trees and random forests requires not only technical knowledge but also a deep understanding of the data and the problem context. Careful preprocessing, feature engineering, and model tuning are necessary to extract the best performance. As machine learning continues to evolve, these tree-based models remain foundational, offering a balance of accuracy, flexibility, and interpretability that is hard to match. Whether used as standalone models or as components in more complex ensembles, decision trees and random forests continue to play a vital role in unlocking the predictive power of data.

Support Vector Machines Explained

Support Vector Machines, commonly referred to as SVMs, are a powerful class of supervised learning algorithms used for classification, regression, and even outlier detection. Their strength lies in their ability to handle high-dimensional data, model complex nonlinear relationships, and maintain robustness even when the number of dimensions exceeds the number of data points. SVMs are particularly effective when dealing with data that is not linearly separable in its original feature space. Through the use of kernel functions, they project data into higher-dimensional spaces where it becomes possible to find clear decision boundaries between classes. Despite their mathematical complexity, the conceptual foundation of SVMs is rooted in a straightforward geometric interpretation, which makes them both elegant and practical.

At the core of a Support Vector Machine for classification is the idea of finding the optimal hyperplane that separates data points from different classes. A hyperplane in a two-dimensional space is a line, in three dimensions it becomes a plane, and in higher dimensions it is a flat affine subspace of one dimension less than the feature space. The optimal hyperplane is the one that not only separates the data points but also maximizes the margin between the closest points of the two classes. These closest data points are called support vectors, and they are critical to defining the decision boundary. Maximizing the margin helps ensure that the model generalizes well to new, unseen data by creating the largest possible separation between classes.

In cases where the data is linearly separable, the SVM finds this maximum-margin hyperplane with a clear mathematical formulation. The optimization problem is convex, which means there is a unique global solution. However, most real-world data is not linearly separable. To handle this, SVMs introduce the concept of soft margins by allowing some misclassifications. This is controlled by a regularization parameter, commonly denoted as C, which balances the trade-off between maximizing the margin and minimizing the classification error. A small value of C creates a wider margin by tolerating more misclassifications, promoting generalization. A large value of C tries to classify every point correctly, potentially at the cost of overfitting.

For data that cannot be effectively separated by a linear boundary, SVMs employ a technique known as the kernel trick. The kernel trick allows the algorithm to operate in a high-dimensional space without explicitly computing the coordinates in that space. Instead, it computes the inner products between the images of all pairs of data points in the feature space, using a kernel function. This approach transforms the problem into one where a linear separator can be found in the transformed space, even if the original data is nonlinearly distributed. Popular kernel functions include the polynomial kernel, radial basis function (RBF) kernel, and sigmoid kernel. Among these, the RBF kernel is particularly widely used because of its ability to handle complex, curved boundaries in the input space.

The choice of kernel and the parameters associated with it play a crucial role in the performance of the SVM. For example, the RBF kernel has a parameter gamma that defines how far the influence of a single training example reaches. A small gamma value results in a smoother decision boundary with broader influence, while a large gamma creates a more complex boundary that fits tightly around the data. Tuning the C and gamma parameters is essential for balancing bias and variance and requires careful cross-validation to identify the combination that delivers the best generalization performance.

In addition to classification, Support Vector Machines can be adapted for regression tasks through a method known as Support Vector Regression (SVR). Instead of finding a hyperplane that separates classes, SVR attempts to fit a function within a margin of tolerance around the true outputs. The goal is to ensure that the predictions fall within a specified epsilon distance from the actual values, while keeping the function as flat as possible. Points outside this margin contribute to the error and are treated similarly to misclassified points in the classification setting. Like its classification counterpart, SVR benefits from kernel functions to model nonlinear relationships and is capable of handling high-dimensional regression problems effectively.

SVMs are also used in anomaly detection, especially in applications where the data from one class is abundant but the data from the other class is rare or unavailable. One-class SVMs are trained only on data from the majority class and learn a decision function that captures the boundary of the normal class. Any new data point falling outside this learned boundary is flagged as an anomaly. This approach is useful in fraud detection, network intrusion detection, and medical diagnostics where anomalies may represent rare but critical events.

Despite their many advantages, SVMs have certain limitations. One of the primary challenges is the computational cost associated with training, especially on large datasets. The algorithm requires solving a quadratic optimization problem, which becomes increasingly resource-intensive as the number of data points grows. Additionally, the choice of kernel and tuning of hyperparameters can be nontrivial and often requires domain expertise and extensive experimentation. SVMs are also less interpretable compared to models like decision trees or linear regression, particularly when complex kernels are used.

Nevertheless, SVMs remain a popular choice for many machine learning practitioners due to their versatility and strong theoretical foundation. They are particularly valuable in applications involving text classification, image recognition, bioinformatics, and other domains where the data is high-dimensional and the relationships between features are complex. Their ability to deliver high accuracy, resist overfitting through margin maximization, and handle nonlinear separability makes them a reliable component of the machine learning toolkit.

When implementing SVMs in practice, it is crucial to preprocess the data appropriately. Feature scaling is particularly important because SVMs are sensitive to the relative magnitudes of the input features. Standardization or normalization helps ensure that all features contribute equally to the distance calculations used by the kernel functions. Additionally, handling imbalanced datasets requires strategies such as class weighting or resampling, as SVMs can be biased toward the majority class.

As data science continues to evolve, SVMs persist as a foundational technique for both research and practical applications. Their unique combination of geometric intuition, mathematical elegance, and empirical effectiveness ensures their relevance across a broad spectrum of machine learning tasks. For practitioners willing to invest time in tuning and understanding the intricacies of the algorithm, Support Vector Machines offer a powerful and adaptable approach to building models that perform well even under challenging conditions.

Clustering Techniques and Applications

Clustering is a fundamental unsupervised learning technique used in data science to discover natural groupings or patterns within a dataset. Unlike supervised learning, where models are trained using labeled data, clustering algorithms operate on datasets without predefined labels or outcomes. The primary objective of clustering is to partition a dataset into groups, or clusters, in such a way that data points within the same cluster are more similar to each other than to those in different clusters. This similarity is typically measured using distance metrics such as Euclidean distance, cosine similarity, or Manhattan distance, depending on the nature of the data and the problem context.

One of the most widely used clustering algorithms is K-means clustering. K-means is a centroid-based algorithm that begins by selecting a predefined number of clusters, denoted as K. It randomly initializes K centroids and assigns each data point to the nearest centroid, forming K clusters. It then updates the centroids by computing the mean of all data points assigned to each cluster. This process of assignment and update is repeated iteratively until the centroids stabilize or a maximum number of iterations is reached. K-means is appreciated for its simplicity and speed, especially on large datasets. However, it requires the number of clusters to be specified in advance and is sensitive to the initial placement of centroids. Additionally, K-means assumes that clusters are spherical and equally sized, which can limit its effectiveness on more complex datasets.

Another popular method is hierarchical clustering, which builds a hierarchy of clusters in a bottom-up or top-down approach. In the agglomerative approach, which is more commonly used, each data point starts as its own cluster. At each iteration, the two closest clusters are merged until all data points are in a single cluster or until a stopping criterion is met. The results of hierarchical clustering are often visualized using a dendrogram, a tree-like diagram that illustrates the order in which clusters are merged. By cutting the dendrogram at a certain level, one can obtain a desired number of clusters. Hierarchical clustering does not require the number of clusters to be specified in advance, and it can capture nested patterns in the data. However, it tends to be computationally expensive and does not scale well to very large datasets.

Density-based clustering methods, such as DBSCAN, take a different approach by identifying regions of high data density. DBSCAN groups together points that are closely packed and labels points that lie alone in low-density regions as outliers. It requires two parameters: epsilon, which defines the radius of a neighborhood, and the minimum number of points required to form a dense region. One of the strengths of DBSCAN is its ability to discover clusters of arbitrary shape and to identify noise in the data. Unlike K-means, it does not assume any particular cluster structure and does not require the number of clusters to be specified beforehand. However, DBSCAN can struggle with datasets of varying density and is sensitive to the choice of its parameters.

Another advancement in clustering is the use of model-based approaches like Gaussian Mixture Models. A GMM assumes that the data is generated from a mixture of several Gaussian distributions, each representing a cluster. It uses the Expectation-Maximization algorithm to estimate the parameters of these distributions and assign probabilities to each data point for belonging to each cluster. This probabilistic approach allows for soft clustering, where data points can belong to multiple clusters with different degrees of membership. GMMs are more flexible than K-means and can model elliptical clusters, but they also assume that the data follows a Gaussian distribution, which may not hold in all cases.

Spectral clustering is another technique that leverages the eigenvalues of similarity matrices to perform dimensionality reduction before applying a clustering algorithm like K-means. This approach is particularly effective when the data is not well-separated in the original feature space but exhibits meaningful structure in a transformed space. Spectral clustering works well with graph-based data and can detect non-convex clusters that would be missed by traditional methods. However, it involves constructing and decomposing a similarity matrix, which can be computationally expensive and sensitive to parameter settings.

Clustering has a wide array of applications across industries. In marketing, it is used for customer segmentation, enabling companies to identify distinct groups of customers based on purchasing behavior, demographics, or engagement metrics. This allows for targeted marketing strategies and personalized recommendations. In healthcare, clustering can help identify patient groups with similar symptoms or responses to treatment, leading to more effective and personalized care plans. In cybersecurity, clustering algorithms can detect anomalous network behavior by identifying groups of similar activity and flagging deviations. In document analysis and natural language processing, clustering is used to organize large collections of text into thematic groups, improving information retrieval and topic discovery.

In image analysis, clustering helps in grouping similar pixels or features, aiding in tasks like object detection and image segmentation. In social network analysis, clustering identifies communities of users who interact more frequently with each other than with the rest of the network. These insights can be used to understand social dynamics, spread of information, or influence propagation. Clustering also plays a role in recommendation systems by grouping users or products with similar preferences and behaviors to improve recommendation accuracy.

Despite its versatility, clustering comes with challenges. Evaluating the quality of clusters is inherently difficult due to the absence of ground truth labels in unsupervised learning. Internal validation metrics such as silhouette score, Davies-Bouldin index, and within-cluster sum of squares assess cluster cohesion and separation. External validation, where available, compares clustering results to known labels using metrics like adjusted Rand index or mutual information. Another challenge is the sensitivity of clustering algorithms to input parameters, feature scaling, and noise in the data. Preprocessing steps such as normalization, dimensionality reduction, and outlier removal are critical to obtaining meaningful clustering results.

Ultimately, the choice of clustering technique depends on the structure of the data, the domain context, and the analytical goals. While no single algorithm works best for every dataset, understanding the strengths and limitations of each method enables practitioners to experiment effectively and interpret results with confidence. Clustering remains a cornerstone of exploratory data analysis, offering a window into the hidden structure of data and enabling data scientists to derive actionable insights in a variety of real-world scenarios.

Dimensionality Reduction with PCA

Dimensionality reduction is a critical aspect of data preprocessing and analysis, particularly when working with high-dimensional datasets. In many real-world applications, data contains a large number of variables, or features, which can lead to complications such as increased computational cost, overfitting, and difficulties in visualization. Principal Component Analysis, or PCA, is one of the most widely used techniques for reducing the number of dimensions in a dataset while preserving as much of the original variability as possible. It achieves this by transforming the data into a new coordinate system, where the greatest variances lie on the first few axes, called principal components.

PCA works by identifying the directions, or axes, in which the data varies the most. These directions are calculated by finding the eigenvectors of the covariance matrix of the dataset. The corresponding eigenvalues indicate the amount of variance explained by each eigenvector. The eigenvectors define the principal components, and they are orthogonal to each other, meaning they are uncorrelated. By selecting the top k principal components that explain the majority of the variance in the data, PCA reduces the dimensionality of the dataset while retaining the most significant information. This transformation helps simplify the dataset, making it easier to analyze and interpret.

The process begins by standardizing the data. Since PCA is sensitive to the scale of the features, it is essential to ensure that each feature contributes equally to the analysis. Standardization involves subtracting the mean and dividing by the standard deviation for each feature, resulting in a dataset with zero mean and unit variance. This step ensures that features measured on different scales do not dominate the principal components simply due to their magnitude. Once the data is standardized, the covariance matrix is computed to examine the relationships between features. This matrix forms the basis for identifying the principal components.

After calculating the covariance matrix, the next step is to compute its eigenvectors and eigenvalues. The eigenvectors determine the directions of the new feature space, while the eigenvalues measure the magnitude of variance captured along each direction. These eigenvectors are then sorted in descending order based on their corresponding eigenvalues. The top eigenvectors are selected to form a transformation matrix, which is used to project the original data into the lower-dimensional space. The result is a new set of features, known as principal components, which represent linear combinations of the original features.

One of the key advantages of PCA is its ability to uncover the intrinsic structure of the data by revealing correlations and patterns that may not be visible in the original feature space. By examining the loadings of the principal components, which indicate the contribution of each original feature to the component, analysts can gain insights into the relationships among variables. This understanding is valuable for feature selection, data visualization, and interpretation. For instance, in a dataset with hundreds of variables, PCA can reduce the complexity to a handful of components that capture the essence of the data, allowing for clearer visualization and more efficient modeling.

In practice, the number of components to retain is a crucial decision in PCA. One common approach is to look at the cumulative explained variance ratio, which shows how much of the total variance is captured by the first k components. A scree plot is often used to visualize the eigenvalues and determine the point at which adding more components yields diminishing returns. Typically, a threshold such as 90 to 95 percent of explained variance is used to decide how many components to keep. This trade-off between dimensionality reduction and information loss is central to the effectiveness of PCA.

PCA is particularly useful in applications involving image compression, genomics, finance, and any field dealing with high-dimensional data. In image processing, PCA can reduce the number of pixels used to represent an image while preserving essential features, thereby lowering storage requirements and improving computational efficiency. In genomics, where datasets often contain thousands of gene expression levels, PCA helps identify underlying genetic patterns and biological markers. In finance, PCA is used to analyze the co-movement of asset prices and to construct portfolios based on underlying market factors. These applications demonstrate PCA's versatility and power in extracting meaningful structure from complex datasets.

Despite its strengths, PCA has limitations. Since it is a linear method, it may not perform well when the relationships among variables are nonlinear. In such cases, alternative techniques like kernel PCA or t-distributed Stochastic Neighbor Embedding may be more appropriate. PCA also assumes that the directions of maximum variance are the most informative, which may not always hold true, especially if the variance is due to noise. Furthermore, the principal components are abstract linear combinations of the original features, which can make them difficult to interpret in a domain-specific context.

Implementing PCA in modern data science tools is straightforward. Libraries such as scikit-learn in Python provide efficient functions to perform PCA with just a few lines of code. The implementation includes options for automatic scaling, setting the number of components, and plotting explained variance. Once the data has been transformed, the new components can be used as input for other machine learning algorithms, reducing model complexity and improving generalization. PCA often serves as a preprocessing step before clustering, classification, or regression, especially when dealing with sparse or noisy data.

In addition to its use in reducing dimensionality, PCA also plays a role in anomaly detection. By projecting data into a lower-dimensional space, PCA can highlight observations that do not conform to the general pattern. These outliers appear as points with unusually large projection errors, indicating potential anomalies. This application is valuable in fields such as fraud detection, network security, and industrial monitoring, where identifying rare and unusual events is critical.

PCA remains a cornerstone of exploratory data analysis and feature engineering. It provides a systematic way to reduce the complexity of high-dimensional data while preserving its essential structure. By leveraging the mathematical properties of variance and orthogonality, PCA offers both a practical tool and a conceptual framework for understanding data. Whether used for visualization, noise reduction, or modeling, PCA enables analysts to work more effectively with complex datasets, revealing patterns and structures that drive insights and decisions. Its combination of simplicity, interpretability, and effectiveness ensures that it continues to be an essential technique in the data scientist's toolkit.

Model Selection and Cross-Validation

Model selection is a central task in the machine learning process, where the goal is to identify the most appropriate algorithm and configuration that yields the best performance on a given dataset. Choosing the right model involves more than simply comparing accuracy scores; it requires a structured approach to evaluating how different models generalize to unseen data. This process becomes even more critical when there are multiple candidate algorithms or when tuning hyperparameters, as overfitting or underfitting can significantly affect predictive performance. A poorly chosen model may perform exceptionally well on training data but fail miserably on new observations. Therefore, model selection must be supported by rigorous validation techniques that provide an unbiased assessment of model quality.

Cross-validation is one of the most robust and widely used methods for assessing a model's generalization ability. The idea behind cross-validation is to divide the data into multiple subsets, or folds, and use different combinations of these subsets for training and testing. The most common form is k-fold cross-validation, where the data is split into k equal parts. The model is trained k times, each time leaving out one of the k folds as the test set and using the remaining k minus one folds for training. The performance metrics are then averaged over the k iterations to provide a more reliable estimate of the model's effectiveness on unseen data. This approach reduces the variance associated with random train-test splits and ensures that every observation is used for both training and validation.

Another variant is stratified k-fold cross-validation, which is especially useful in classification problems involving imbalanced classes. Stratification ensures that each fold has a representative distribution of the target classes, avoiding scenarios where a particular class is absent from the validation set. This improves the reliability of performance estimates and avoids misleading conclusions about model accuracy. Leave-one-out cross-validation is an extreme case of k-fold where k equals the number of observations, meaning the model is trained on all but one observation and tested on the excluded instance. While this method provides very thorough validation, it is computationally expensive and rarely used in large datasets.

When selecting a model, it is not enough to compare models based on a single metric. Different models may excel in different aspects, and the choice of evaluation metric depends on the problem context. In classification, metrics such as accuracy, precision, recall, F1-score, and AUC-ROC are considered, while in regression, metrics like mean squared error, mean absolute error, and R-squared are used. Cross-validation allows these metrics to be calculated multiple times across different data splits, providing a distribution of scores that reflects the model's stability and robustness. This distribution is more informative than a single point estimate and highlights how sensitive a model is to changes in the data.

Hyperparameter tuning is closely tied to model selection. Many machine learning algorithms have parameters that are not learned from the data but must be set before the training process begins. Examples include the regularization strength in logistic regression, the depth of a decision tree, or the learning rate in gradient boosting. Selecting the optimal combination of hyperparameters can significantly affect model performance. Cross-validation is an essential tool in this tuning process, typically performed using techniques such as grid search or randomized search. Grid search involves systematically evaluating all possible combinations of a predefined set of hyperparameters, while randomized search samples a random subset of combinations and is often more efficient, especially when the hyperparameter space is large.

To avoid overfitting during model selection and hyperparameter tuning, nested cross-validation is often employed. In nested cross-validation, the data is split into outer and inner folds. The inner folds are used for hyperparameter tuning, while the outer folds are used to assess the performance of the model with the best parameters. This approach prevents information leakage from the validation set into the model training process and provides a more honest estimate of how the final model will perform on new data. Nested cross-validation is particularly important when working with small datasets, where the risk of overfitting is higher.

Another consideration during model selection is computational efficiency. Some models, while highly accurate, may require significant time and resources to train and predict. In production environments where response time and scalability are critical, a slightly less accurate but faster model might be preferred. Cross-validation provides insight into both the performance and consistency of models, enabling informed trade-offs between accuracy and efficiency. Models that perform well across all folds with low variance in metrics are typically more reliable than models with highly variable results.

Ensemble methods often come into play during model selection. Techniques like bagging, boosting, and stacking combine multiple models to improve overall performance. In such cases, cross-validation helps determine the best way to combine base models or select the right base learners. For example, stacking uses a meta-model to blend the predictions of several base models. The base models are trained on the training data, and their predictions on validation folds are used to train the meta-model. Cross-validation ensures that this layering process does not introduce bias or overfitting.

The final step after selecting and validating the best model is to train it on the entire dataset before deployment. This ensures that the model benefits from all available data while preserving the knowledge gained from the cross-validation process. It is important to document the results of the cross-validation, including the chosen model, the hyperparameter values, the evaluation metrics, and the standard deviation of performance across folds. This transparency supports reproducibility and allows for future audits or improvements.

Model selection and cross-validation form the backbone of a reliable machine learning pipeline. They enable practitioners to make informed decisions grounded in data rather than intuition. By rigorously evaluating models and avoiding overfitting traps, data scientists ensure that their solutions are not only accurate but also generalizable and robust. In an era where data-driven decisions carry significant consequences, this disciplined approach to model development is more important than ever. Through careful model selection and systematic validation, machine learning models can achieve high performance while maintaining the trust and confidence of stakeholders.

Hyperparameter Tuning and Optimization

Hyperparameter tuning and optimization are critical components in the development of high-performing machine learning models. Hyperparameters are parameters that govern the training process of an algorithm and must be set before training begins. Unlike model parameters, which are learned from the data during the training phase, hyperparameters control aspects such as the complexity of the model, the speed of learning, the structure of the model, and regularization. Selecting the right combination of hyperparameters can mean the difference between a model that generalizes well to unseen data and one that either underfits or overfits. Because hyperparameters are not directly learned, they require external strategies to be fine-tuned through experimentation and validation.

The process of hyperparameter tuning involves defining a search space, which is the range of possible values for each hyperparameter, and then using a search strategy to explore this space. The most straightforward method is grid search, where a predefined set of values is specified for each hyperparameter and the algorithm evaluates every possible combination of these values. Although exhaustive, grid search can be extremely time-consuming, especially as the number of hyperparameters and their possible values increases. Its performance is limited by the curse of dimensionality, as the number of evaluations grows exponentially with the number of parameters. Despite its simplicity, grid search remains popular for small-scale problems and provides a baseline for comparison with more sophisticated methods.

Random search offers an alternative to grid search by sampling combinations of hyperparameter values at random. Rather than testing every possible configuration, it explores the space stochastically and often identifies good combinations with fewer evaluations. Studies have shown that random search can be more efficient than grid search, particularly when some hyperparameters are more influential than others. By focusing the search on a broader portion of the hyperparameter space rather than systematically exploring all combinations, random search increases the chances of finding a near-optimal configuration in less time.

Bayesian optimization represents a more advanced approach to hyperparameter tuning. It builds a probabilistic model of the objective function, often using Gaussian processes, and chooses the next set of hyperparameters to evaluate based on expected improvement. The key idea is to balance exploration of unknown regions of the space with exploitation of areas known to produce good results. Bayesian optimization is particularly useful when model training is computationally expensive, as it seeks to minimize the number of evaluations required to find an optimal set of hyperparameters. Although more complex to implement, it offers significant advantages in efficiency and performance, especially when combined with parallel computing resources.

Another strategy involves the use of gradient-based optimization for hyperparameters. In some advanced techniques, such as in neural architecture search or differentiable hyperparameter tuning, gradients can be computed with respect to hyperparameters. These methods are generally more experimental and computationally demanding, but they represent the cutting edge of research in automated machine learning. Evolutionary algorithms, such as genetic algorithms, also play a role in hyperparameter tuning by simulating natural selection processes to evolve sets of hyperparameters over successive generations. These algorithms use mechanisms like mutation, crossover, and selection to iteratively refine the population of candidate solutions.

When conducting hyperparameter tuning, it is essential to use a robust validation strategy to assess the performance of each configuration. Cross-validation is widely employed to ensure that the performance estimate is reliable and not biased by a particular train-test split. For example, in k-fold cross-validation, the dataset is divided into k subsets, and the model is trained k times, each time leaving out one fold for validation. The performance scores are averaged to provide a more general estimate. Nested cross-validation is used when hyperparameter tuning is combined with model evaluation to avoid data leakage and overfitting. In nested cross-validation, one loop is used for tuning and another for evaluating the best configuration.

Automated machine learning platforms have integrated hyperparameter optimization as a core feature, allowing data scientists to focus more on problem formulation and interpretation rather than manual experimentation. Tools such as Optuna, Hyperopt, and Scikit-Optimize provide frameworks for defining search spaces and applying sophisticated optimization algorithms. These tools support pruning of unpromising trials, early stopping, and parallel execution, making them highly efficient in practice. Additionally, cloud-based machine learning services offer managed hyperparameter tuning that leverages large-scale distributed infrastructure to accelerate the search process.

Hyperparameter tuning is not only about finding the best model performance on a validation set; it is also about achieving a balance between complexity and generalization. Over-optimized models can perform well on validation data but fail on truly unseen test data, particularly when the tuning process inadvertently captures noise or artifacts specific to the validation set. Therefore, a final evaluation on a separate test set is crucial before deploying the model into production. Logging and monitoring during tuning are also essential for reproducibility, accountability, and model governance. Keeping track of which configurations were tested, along with their associated performance metrics and computational costs, enables better understanding and future improvement.

The choice of hyperparameters varies across algorithms. In decision trees and random forests, key hyperparameters include the maximum depth of the tree, the minimum number of samples per split, and the number of trees in the ensemble. In support vector machines, the regularization parameter C and the kernel parameters such as gamma must be carefully tuned. In gradient boosting machines, learning rate, number of boosting rounds, and tree-specific parameters play a significant role. For neural networks, the number of layers, number of units per layer, activation functions, batch size, and optimization algorithms form a vast space of tunable parameters. Each algorithm has its own sensitivities, and a deep understanding of these relationships enhances the effectiveness of tuning.

Hyperparameter tuning is a time-intensive but necessary step in the creation of robust and high-performing models. It requires not just technical know-how but also a strategic mindset to allocate resources wisely and to avoid overfitting. The increasing availability of automated tools and distributed computing resources has made hyperparameter optimization more accessible, enabling data scientists to explore more complex models and deliver better results. Nonetheless, human intuition and domain expertise remain invaluable in defining search spaces, interpreting results, and making final decisions. As machine learning continues to grow in scale and impact, efficient and intelligent hyperparameter tuning will remain at the core of model development and deployment.

Working with Imbalanced Data

Imbalanced data presents one of the most persistent and challenging problems in machine learning. It occurs when the distribution of classes in a dataset is significantly skewed, meaning that one class contains far more observations than the other. This is common in many real-world scenarios such as fraud detection, medical diagnosis, rare event prediction, and churn analysis. In such cases, the minority class is typically the most important, as it represents the event or outcome that practitioners aim to detect or prevent. However, standard machine learning algorithms tend to perform poorly on imbalanced datasets because they are optimized to maximize overall accuracy and therefore favor the majority class. This bias can result in models that appear to perform well in aggregate but fail to correctly identify critical minority class instances.

A fundamental issue with imbalanced data is that traditional evaluation metrics such as accuracy can be misleading. For example, if only one percent of the observations belong to the minority class, a naive model that predicts only the majority class would achieve ninety-nine percent accuracy but have no practical value. More appropriate metrics in these cases include precision, recall, F_1-score, and area under the precision-recall curve. These metrics provide a better understanding of how well the model performs in detecting the minority class, especially when the cost of false negatives is high. For instance, in medical applications, failing to detect a disease can have far more severe consequences than incorrectly diagnosing a healthy patient.

Addressing imbalanced data requires a combination of data-level and algorithm-level strategies. At the data level, resampling techniques are commonly used to balance the class distribution. Oversampling increases the number of minority class samples, while undersampling reduces the number of majority class samples. One of the most popular oversampling methods is Synthetic Minority Over-sampling Technique (SMOTE), which generates synthetic examples of the minority class by interpolating between existing examples. This helps in creating a more balanced training set without simply duplicating data, which could lead to overfitting. Undersampling, on the other hand, can be effective in reducing training time and simplifying the model, but it risks discarding potentially valuable information from the majority class.

More advanced variations of SMOTE, such as Borderline-SMOTE and ADASYN, focus on generating synthetic samples in regions where the minority and majority classes overlap. These methods aim to strengthen the decision boundary by emphasizing harder-to-classify examples. Similarly, ensemble approaches like SMOTE combined with bagging can be used to create multiple balanced training subsets, each contributing to a final model that generalizes better. Care must be taken when applying oversampling and undersampling, especially in small datasets, to avoid introducing noise or eliminating meaningful variance.

Algorithm-level strategies involve modifying existing algorithms or using models that are inherently more robust to class imbalance. Many machine learning libraries allow for class weighting, where the loss function penalizes misclassification of the minority class more heavily. This encourages the model to pay more attention to minority class examples. For instance, in logistic regression or support vector machines, assigning higher weights to the minority class can significantly improve recall without drastically reducing precision. Tree-based algorithms like Random Forest and Gradient Boosting Machines often include built-in mechanisms for handling imbalance through class weights or customized loss functions.

Another technique involves threshold moving, where the classification threshold is adjusted to improve the detection of the minority class. By default, many classifiers use a threshold of 0.5 for binary classification, meaning predictions above 0.5 are assigned to the positive class. However, this threshold can be shifted to favor the minority class, thereby increasing recall at the cost of precision. This is particularly useful when the cost of missing a minority class instance is higher than making a false positive. Precision-recall trade-offs can be visualized using precision-recall curves or ROC curves, which help in selecting the optimal threshold based on domain-specific needs.

Cost-sensitive learning is another approach where the learning algorithm incorporates the cost of different types of misclassification directly into the model. This is especially useful in applications where the consequences of errors are not uniform. For example, in fraud detection, failing to identify a fraudulent transaction could result in significant financial loss, whereas flagging a legitimate transaction might only cause a temporary inconvenience. Designing a model that takes these costs into account during training leads to more practical and application-oriented outcomes.

Working with imbalanced data also involves careful cross-validation to ensure that the performance estimates are accurate and meaningful.

Standard k-fold cross-validation may not maintain the class distribution in each fold, leading to biased results. Stratified k-fold cross-validation addresses this by preserving the proportion of classes in each fold, ensuring that both the training and validation sets reflect the original imbalance. This provides more consistent and realistic assessments of model performance.

Visualization plays an important role in understanding the effects of imbalance and the behavior of the classifier. Confusion matrices, precision-recall curves, and class distribution plots help diagnose problems and inform strategy adjustments. Visual inspection can reveal whether the model is overly confident in majority class predictions or whether it fails to identify minority class examples in ambiguous regions of the feature space.

Finally, domain knowledge is essential in guiding decisions about how to handle imbalanced data. Understanding the real-world implications of different types of errors allows data scientists to prioritize objectives and select the most appropriate methods. Collaboration with domain experts ensures that the chosen metrics, thresholds, and modeling approaches align with the actual goals and constraints of the application. This context-driven approach transforms imbalanced data from a technical obstacle into a manageable and strategically important challenge.

By integrating thoughtful preprocessing, tailored algorithmic adjustments, and domain-aware evaluation strategies, models can be trained to perform well even in the face of severe class imbalance. The goal is not merely to balance numbers but to build systems that recognize and prioritize the rare and critical cases that matter most. As imbalanced datasets are the norm rather than the exception in many practical applications, mastering the tools and techniques to handle them effectively is a vital skill for any data scientist.

Introduction to Deep Learning

Deep learning is a subfield of machine learning that focuses on algorithms inspired by the structure and function of the human brain, particularly neural networks. It has revolutionized fields such as computer vision, natural language processing, speech recognition, and game playing, achieving state-of-the-art performance in many tasks that were previously thought to be beyond the capabilities of machines. At its core, deep learning involves training models with multiple layers of abstraction that can learn complex patterns and representations from large amounts of data. The term deep refers to the presence of multiple layers in a neural network, each of which learns a different level of abstraction from the input data.

The foundation of deep learning lies in the artificial neural network, a computational model composed of layers of interconnected nodes or neurons. Each neuron receives input from other neurons or from the raw data, processes this input using a mathematical function, and then passes the result to the next layer. The basic structure of a neural network includes an input layer, one or more hidden layers, and an output layer. During training, the network adjusts the weights of the connections between neurons to minimize the error between its predictions and the actual targets. This is done using a technique called backpropagation combined with an optimization algorithm like stochastic gradient descent.

Deep learning models are particularly well suited for tasks involving unstructured data such as images, audio, and text. In traditional machine learning, significant effort is required to manually engineer features that capture the relevant information in the data. Deep learning, by contrast, automates much of this process by learning hierarchical features directly from the raw input. For example, in an image recognition task, the early layers of a convolutional neural network might learn to detect edges and simple shapes, while deeper layers learn to recognize parts of objects and ultimately entire objects themselves. This ability to automatically learn rich representations makes deep learning extremely powerful.

Training deep neural networks requires large datasets and substantial computational resources. The rise of big data and advances in hardware, particularly graphics processing units, have been key factors in the success of deep learning. GPUs are well suited for the matrix and tensor operations that underlie neural network computations, enabling the training of models with millions of parameters in a reasonable amount of time. In addition, software frameworks such as TensorFlow and PyTorch have made it easier for researchers and practitioners to build, train, and deploy deep learning models.

There are several types of deep learning architectures, each designed for specific types of tasks. Feedforward neural networks, also known as multilayer perceptrons, are the simplest type and consist of layers where data flows in one direction from input to output. These networks are suitable for tasks where the data is static and of fixed size. Convolutional neural networks are specialized for processing grid-like data such as images. They use convolutional layers that apply filters to local regions of the input, capturing spatial hierarchies and patterns. CNNs have been remarkably successful in tasks such as image classification, object detection, and medical image analysis.

Recurrent neural networks are designed for sequential data, where the order of the data points matters. RNNs have connections that form cycles, allowing information to persist across time steps. This makes them suitable for tasks like time series forecasting, speech recognition, and natural language modeling. However, standard RNNs suffer from issues such as vanishing gradients, which limit their ability to learn long-range dependencies. To address this, variants like Long Short-Term Memory and Gated Recurrent Units have been developed. These architectures introduce gating mechanisms that help maintain information over longer sequences.

Another major breakthrough in deep learning has been the development of transformer architectures, which have rapidly become the dominant approach in natural language processing. Transformers rely on a mechanism called self-attention, which allows the model to weigh the importance of different words in a sentence when making predictions. Unlike RNNs, transformers can process all elements of a sequence in parallel, making them more efficient and scalable. Models such as BERT, GPT, and T5 have set new benchmarks on a wide range of language understanding and generation tasks, from machine translation to question answering.

Despite their impressive capabilities, deep learning models are not without limitations. They are often considered black boxes due to their complex internal workings, making it difficult to interpret how decisions are made. This lack of transparency can be problematic in high-stakes domains such as healthcare, finance, and law, where explainability and trust are essential. Research in the field of explainable AI seeks to address this by developing techniques that provide insights into model behavior, such as visualizing activations or attributing predictions to specific inputs.

Overfitting is another challenge in deep learning, especially when the model is too complex relative to the amount of training data. Regularization techniques such as dropout, weight decay, and data augmentation help prevent overfitting by reducing the model's capacity or introducing noise during training. Careful design of the model architecture, along with proper tuning of hyperparameters, is crucial to achieving good generalization. The use of validation sets and cross-validation ensures that the model performs well not just on the training data but also on unseen examples.

Transfer learning has emerged as a powerful approach to make deep learning more accessible and efficient. It involves taking a model that has been pre-trained on a large dataset and fine-tuning it on a smaller, task-specific dataset. This reduces the need for extensive training data and computational resources while often leading to better performance. In computer vision, pre-trained CNNs such as ResNet or VGG are frequently used as starting points for custom classification tasks. In NLP, models like BERT and GPT can be fine-tuned for a wide variety of applications with minimal changes.

Deep learning continues to evolve rapidly, with ongoing research pushing the boundaries of what machines can learn and do. New architectures, training methods, and applications are constantly emerging, expanding the scope and impact of this technology. From autonomous vehicles and voice assistants to medical diagnostics and creative tools, deep learning is reshaping industries and redefining possibilities. As the field matures, the focus is increasingly shifting toward making deep learning models more interpretable, fair, and energy efficient, ensuring that their benefits can be widely shared and responsibly deployed in real-world settings. Understanding the fundamentals of deep learning equips practitioners with the knowledge to harness its power and contribute to its continued advancement.

Neural Networks and Backpropagation

Neural networks are the foundational building blocks of deep learning, designed to mimic the way the human brain processes information. They consist of layers of interconnected nodes called neurons, each of which performs a simple computation. These networks are capable of approximating complex nonlinear functions and learning intricate patterns from data. At their core, neural networks learn to map inputs to outputs by adjusting the strengths, or weights, of the connections between neurons. The learning process relies heavily on an algorithm known as backpropagation, which allows the network to update its weights systematically in order to minimize the difference between its predictions and the actual outcomes.

A basic neural network is composed of an input layer, one or more hidden layers, and an output layer. Each neuron receives input signals, applies a weighted sum, adds a bias, and then passes the result through an activation function. This activation function introduces nonlinearity into the model, enabling the network to learn and represent complex relationships. Common activation functions include the sigmoid, hyperbolic tangent, and the rectified linear unit. The rectified linear unit, or ReLU, has become especially popular in modern deep learning due to its computational efficiency and ability to mitigate the vanishing gradient problem.

When a neural network is initialized, its weights are typically set to small random values. During the forward pass, input data is fed through the network, and the outputs are computed layer by layer until the final prediction is made. This prediction is then compared to the actual target value using a loss function, which quantifies the error. The choice of loss function depends on the type of task being performed. For regression problems, mean squared error is commonly used, while classification tasks often use cross-entropy loss. Once the loss is calculated, the network needs to adjust its weights to reduce this error. This is where backpropagation comes into play.

Backpropagation is a training algorithm that computes the gradient of the loss function with respect to each weight in the network by applying the chain rule of calculus. It proceeds in the reverse direction of the forward pass, starting from the output layer and moving backward through the network. The gradients indicate how much the loss would change if a particular weight were changed slightly. These gradients are then used by an optimization algorithm, such as stochastic gradient descent, to update the weights in a direction that reduces the loss. This iterative process continues over multiple passes through the training data, known as epochs, gradually improving the network's performance.

One of the strengths of backpropagation is its efficiency in training networks with many layers and parameters. It enables deep neural networks to learn meaningful internal representations of data, transforming raw inputs into features that are useful for making predictions. However, training deep networks is not without challenges. One of the most common issues is the vanishing gradient problem, where gradients become extremely small as they are propagated backward through the layers. This makes it difficult for weights in earlier layers to update effectively, slowing down learning or causing it to stall altogether. Techniques such as using ReLU activations, batch normalization, and residual connections have been developed to address this issue and facilitate the training of deeper networks.

Weight initialization also plays a critical role in the effectiveness of backpropagation. Poor initialization can lead to exploding gradients or cause neurons to become inactive. Modern initialization strategies, such as Xavier or He initialization, are designed to keep the variance of activations and gradients stable across layers. Additionally, the choice of optimizer significantly impacts the convergence of training. While standard stochastic gradient descent updates weights based on the average gradient over small batches of data, variants like Adam, RMSprop, and AdaGrad incorporate adaptive learning rates and momentum to accelerate convergence and navigate complex loss surfaces more effectively.

Regularization is another important aspect of training neural networks. Since networks with many parameters can easily overfit the training data, techniques such as L1 and L2 regularization, dropout, and early stopping are employed to improve generalization. Dropout works by randomly disabling a fraction of the neurons during each training step, forcing the network to learn redundant representations and reducing reliance on specific paths through the network. Early stopping monitors the performance of the model on a validation set and halts training when the validation error stops improving, preventing the model from continuing to memorize the training data.

Neural networks can be extended and adapted for various types of data and tasks. Convolutional neural networks are tailored for spatial data such as images, using convolutional layers to detect local patterns. Recurrent neural networks are designed for sequential data, maintaining internal states that capture temporal dependencies. More recent architectures, like transformers, use attention mechanisms to model relationships in data without relying on sequential processing. All of these architectures rely fundamentally on the principles of forward propagation and backpropagation, highlighting the centrality of these concepts in deep learning.

Visualization of the training process can provide valuable insights into how well backpropagation is working. Plotting the loss curve over time can reveal whether the model is learning steadily or has plateaued. Examining the gradients can indicate whether vanishing or exploding gradients are occurring. Visualizing the weights and activations can help understand which features the network is focusing on and whether certain neurons are being underutilized. These tools aid in diagnosing problems and guiding adjustments to the network architecture or training procedure.

Backpropagation has enabled neural networks to achieve remarkable success across a wide range of applications. In computer vision, networks trained with backpropagation can recognize objects, detect faces, and interpret medical images with superhuman accuracy. In natural language processing, they power machine translation, sentiment analysis, and conversational agents. In gaming and reinforcement learning, backpropagation is used to train agents that can master complex environments through trial and error. The versatility and power of neural networks stem largely from their ability to learn representations automatically, and backpropagation is the engine that drives this learning process.

Understanding neural networks and backpropagation is essential for anyone working in artificial intelligence or data science. These concepts form the foundation upon which modern deep learning systems are built. They embody the idea that complex tasks can be solved by composing many simple functions and refining them through feedback. As models grow in scale and complexity, the principles of neural computation and gradient-based optimization continue to be at the heart of technological progress in intelligent systems. The journey from a random collection of weights to a trained model capable of solving real-world problems is made possible by the elegant and powerful mechanism of backpropagation.

Convolutional Neural Networks for Images

Convolutional Neural Networks, or CNNs, are a specialized type of neural network designed specifically for processing data with a grid-like topology, such as images. Unlike traditional fully connected neural networks where every input is connected to every neuron in the next layer, CNNs leverage a local connectivity structure that significantly reduces the number of parameters and enhances their ability to capture spatial hierarchies in data. This design makes CNNs exceptionally effective for visual tasks, including image classification, object detection, segmentation, facial recognition, and medical imaging diagnostics. The architecture of a CNN reflects the way human vision processes information, starting with the detection of simple patterns like edges and progressing to more complex features as the network deepens.

The fundamental building block of a CNN is the convolutional layer, which applies filters, also called kernels, to small patches of the input image. These filters slide across the input in a process called convolution, computing dot products between the filter values and the input values in the receptive field. Each filter is designed to detect specific features such as edges, corners, textures, or other spatial patterns. As a result, the output of a convolutional layer, known as a feature map or activation map, highlights the presence of these features across the spatial dimensions of the input. During training, the filters learn to recognize the most informative features for the given task, making the network capable of learning directly from raw pixel data without manual feature extraction.

After each convolutional layer, it is common to apply a nonlinear activation function such as the rectified linear unit. ReLU introduces nonlinearity to the network, allowing it to learn more complex mappings from inputs to outputs. Without such nonlinear functions, no matter how many layers the network has, it would still behave like a linear model. ReLU is particularly favored for its simplicity and effectiveness in mitigating the vanishing gradient problem, which often hampers the training of deep neural networks.

In addition to convolution and activation layers, pooling layers are a key component of CNNs. Pooling is a downsampling operation that reduces the spatial dimensions of the feature maps, thereby lowering the computational load and controlling overfitting. The most common type of pooling is max pooling, which selects the maximum value within each sub-region of the feature map. This operation helps retain the most prominent features while discarding less relevant details, contributing to translational invariance, which is the ability of the network to recognize objects regardless of their location in the image.

CNNs are typically composed of multiple convolutional and pooling layers stacked together, followed by one or more fully connected layers at the end. The final layers aggregate the high-level features detected in the earlier layers and use them to perform classification or regression. In classification tasks, the output layer often uses a softmax activation function to produce a probability distribution over the predefined classes. The class with the highest probability is selected as the model's prediction. During training, a loss function such as categorical cross-entropy measures the difference between the predicted and actual class labels, and backpropagation is used to update the weights throughout the network to minimize this loss.

One of the strengths of CNNs lies in their parameter sharing and local connectivity, which not only reduce the number of trainable parameters compared to fully connected networks but also enable the model to be more data-efficient. This is particularly important in image processing tasks where the input size can be extremely large. For example, a 256x256 image with three color channels has nearly 200,000 input features. Training a fully connected network on such data would require an enormous number of weights, making it computationally impractical and prone to overfitting. CNNs, by focusing on local patterns and reusing filters across the image, provide a much more scalable and effective solution.

Modern CNN architectures have evolved significantly and now include advanced components and design principles. Architectures like AlexNet, VGGNet, GoogLeNet, ResNet, and DenseNet have set new benchmarks in image recognition challenges. AlexNet introduced deep convolutional layers and popularized the use of GPUs for training. VGGNet demonstrated the power of using small 3x3 filters and a uniform architecture. GoogLeNet introduced the inception module to improve computational efficiency. ResNet addressed the problem of training very deep networks by introducing skip connections, allowing gradients to flow more effectively during backpropagation. These innovations have pushed the boundaries of what CNNs can achieve, enabling them to learn more detailed and abstract representations.

Data augmentation is often used in conjunction with CNNs to enhance model generalization. By applying transformations such as rotation, flipping, scaling, and cropping to the training images, new variations are created, exposing the model to a broader range of inputs. This helps prevent overfitting and improves the robustness of the model. Additionally, techniques like dropout, batch normalization, and weight regularization are employed during training to stabilize learning and encourage better generalization to unseen data.

Transfer learning has also become a widely adopted approach in image-related tasks. It involves using a pre-trained CNN, such as ResNet or Inception, which has been trained on a large dataset like ImageNet, and adapting it to a new task. This is achieved either by fine-tuning the entire network on the new data or by using the pre-trained network as a fixed feature extractor and training only the final layers. Transfer learning is especially valuable when the available labeled data is limited, as it allows the model to leverage previously learned visual representations, accelerating training and often leading to improved performance.

CNNs have also found applications beyond traditional image classification. In object detection, models like YOLO and Faster R-CNN not only classify images but also locate objects within them using bounding boxes. In semantic segmentation, CNNs assign a label to each pixel, allowing detailed understanding of image content. Medical imaging applications use CNNs to detect tumors, classify tissue types, and assist in diagnostics. In the field of autonomous driving, CNNs are employed for lane detection, pedestrian recognition, and obstacle avoidance. The versatility and performance of CNNs make them an indispensable tool in the field of computer vision.

The continued evolution of convolutional neural networks is being driven by innovations in architecture, optimization techniques, and hardware capabilities. Researchers are exploring novel ideas such as attention mechanisms, hybrid models, and neural architecture search to further enhance the capabilities of CNNs. As the demand for automated visual understanding grows, from smartphones and social media to industrial inspection and scientific discovery, CNNs will remain at the forefront of machine learning applications. Understanding their structure, operation, and best practices is essential for any practitioner working in the realm of visual data.

Recurrent Neural Networks for Sequences

Recurrent Neural Networks, or RNNs, are a class of neural networks specifically designed to process sequential data. Unlike traditional feedforward neural networks that assume inputs are independent of one another, RNNs are built to recognize patterns across time steps by maintaining a form of memory. This makes them highly suitable for tasks where the order and context of the data matter, such as time series forecasting, natural language processing, speech recognition, and music generation. The key innovation of RNNs lies in their ability to retain information from previous inputs and use it to influence the processing of current and future inputs, thereby enabling temporal and contextual learning.

An RNN consists of a chain-like architecture where each element in the sequence is processed by a repeating unit, or cell, that passes information to the next step. Each cell receives input data for the current time step and also takes in the hidden state from the previous cell, which serves as its memory. The hidden state acts as a summary of all the past information the network has seen so far, allowing it to build up a contextual understanding over time. During the forward pass, each input in the sequence contributes to the evolution of the hidden state, and in tasks like language modeling or sequence prediction, the final output is derived from the hidden states.

The mathematical formulation of an RNN cell involves applying a transformation to both the current input and the previous hidden state, typically followed by a non-linear activation function such as tanh or ReLU. This results in a new hidden state, which is then passed on to the next time step. The parameters used in this transformation, including weight matrices and biases, are shared across all time steps, which significantly reduces the number of parameters and enables the model to generalize across different positions in the sequence. Despite their conceptual simplicity, training RNNs effectively presents significant challenges.

One of the most well-known issues in training RNNs is the problem of vanishing and exploding gradients. Because the gradients are propagated backward through time using backpropagation through time, or BPTT, they can either shrink exponentially or grow uncontrollably with the number of time steps. When gradients vanish, the network struggles to learn long-range dependencies, which are critical for understanding context in lengthy sequences. When they explode, the training becomes unstable and erratic. This problem limits the ability of basic RNNs to capture long-term information, making them less effective for complex sequence modeling tasks.

To overcome these limitations, more sophisticated variants of RNNs have been developed. The most prominent among these are the Long Short-Term Memory network, or LSTM, and the Gated Recurrent Unit, or GRU. Both introduce gating mechanisms that regulate the flow of information through the network, allowing the model to retain important information for longer periods while discarding irrelevant details. In LSTMs, each cell contains three gates: the input gate, forget gate, and output gate. These gates control how much of the current input, previous hidden state, and internal cell state should be passed on. GRUs simplify this structure by combining the forget and input gates into a single update gate, making them computationally more efficient while still capturing long-range dependencies effectively.

LSTMs and GRUs have enabled breakthroughs in a variety of sequence modeling applications. In natural language processing, they are used to build language models that predict the next word in a sentence, machine translation systems that convert text from one language to another, and sentiment analysis models that interpret the emotional tone of a text. In speech recognition, RNNs help transcribe spoken language into text by processing audio features over time. In time series forecasting, they model financial data, sensor readings, and other temporal signals to predict future values. Their ability to handle sequences of varying length and to learn dependencies across different time scales makes them versatile tools in any domain involving sequential data.

Despite their success, RNNs have some limitations compared to newer architectures. They process sequences step by step, which prevents parallelization and makes them slower to train. They also tend to be sensitive to the choice of hyperparameters, requiring careful tuning of learning rates, sequence lengths, and network depth. Regularization techniques such as dropout, gradient clipping, and layer normalization are often necessary to stabilize training and improve generalization. Bidirectional RNNs are another extension that enhances performance by processing sequences in both forward and backward directions, thereby capturing context from both past and future states.

In recent years, attention mechanisms have been introduced to augment or replace RNNs in many sequence modeling tasks. Attention allows models to focus on specific parts of the input sequence when making predictions, rather than relying solely on a fixed-size hidden state. This has led to the development of transformer models, which do not use recurrence but instead rely entirely on attention to model relationships between sequence elements. Despite the rise of transformers, RNNs, particularly LSTMs and GRUs, remain widely used and relevant due to their efficiency and interpretability in scenarios with limited data or constrained computational resources.

Training RNNs involves using sequences of data as input and computing the loss based on predictions at each time step or at the end of the sequence, depending on the task. This loss is then used to perform backpropagation through time, which unrolls the network across the sequence length and updates the shared parameters. It is important to manage memory and computation carefully during training, especially for long sequences. Techniques such as truncated BPTT, which limits the number of steps over which gradients are backpropagated, are used to reduce computational burden while still capturing useful temporal patterns.

RNNs are also frequently combined with convolutional layers, attention mechanisms, and dense layers to create hybrid architectures suited to specific problems. For example, in video analysis, convolutional layers can extract spatial features from frames while RNNs model the temporal dynamics. In speech synthesis, RNNs can generate audio waveforms from text or feature representations. The modular nature of deep learning frameworks makes it easy to experiment with different configurations and adapt RNNs to diverse use cases.

Understanding and implementing recurrent neural networks provides a strong foundation for sequence modeling. While newer models may offer advantages in some areas, RNNs continue to offer valuable insights into the dynamics of sequential data and remain a key part of the machine learning toolkit. Their ability to remember and process information over time, combined with modern training techniques and architectural innovations, ensures their continued relevance in both research and real-world applications. As technology progresses, RNNs will likely coexist with other models, contributing to the growing capacity of artificial intelligence systems to understand and generate complex sequences of data.

Data Pipelines and Workflow Automation

In the field of data science, building robust, scalable, and maintainable systems is essential for turning raw data into actionable insights. As data volumes grow and become increasingly complex, manual handling of tasks such as data ingestion, transformation, validation, and model training becomes inefficient and error-prone. To address this, data pipelines and workflow automation have become central components in modern data-driven systems. A data pipeline is a series of processes that move data from source to destination, passing through various stages of cleaning, transformation, enrichment, and storage. Workflow automation refers to the orchestration and execution of these processes in a structured and repeatable manner. Together, they provide the backbone for scalable data science and machine learning operations.

Data pipelines are typically composed of several stages, each designed to perform a specific task. The process often begins with data ingestion, where data is collected from diverse sources such as databases, APIs, flat files, streaming platforms, or cloud storage. This stage must handle different formats and protocols, and often requires authentication, batching, and scheduling to ensure that the data arrives reliably and in a timely manner. Once ingested, the data moves to a staging area where it is subjected to validation checks. This includes verifying data types, checking for missing values, detecting anomalies, and ensuring schema consistency. These quality checks are crucial to prevent downstream errors and ensure the integrity of the pipeline.

Following validation, data is typically transformed to a format that is more suitable for analysis or modeling. This transformation step, also known as ETL (Extract, Transform, Load), can involve a wide range of operations such as normalization, aggregation, filtering, feature engineering, and data enrichment. In some cases, it may also include joining datasets from different sources, applying business rules, or anonymizing sensitive information. Efficient implementation of these transformations requires not only programming knowledge but also an understanding of the underlying business logic. The transformed data is then loaded into a data warehouse, data lake, or another storage solution where it becomes available for analytics, reporting, or machine learning.

Automation of these pipelines ensures that the processes run consistently and without manual intervention. Tools such as Apache Airflow, Luigi, Prefect, and Dagster provide frameworks for defining, scheduling, and monitoring workflows. These tools allow developers to represent pipelines as directed acyclic graphs, where each node corresponds to a task and edges define dependencies. By abstracting the workflow logic into reusable components, they make it easier to manage complexity, ensure fault tolerance, and handle retries or conditional execution paths. Logging and alerting features are typically built in, allowing teams to monitor performance and respond quickly to failures.

Workflow automation is especially important in machine learning operations, where models must be trained, evaluated, and deployed regularly to maintain accuracy. Automating the entire model lifecycle, from data preprocessing to model versioning and deployment, allows organizations to maintain continuous integration and continuous delivery practices for machine learning. Pipelines can be configured to retrain models on a scheduled basis or in response to specific events, such as the arrival of new data or the detection of concept drift. This helps ensure that models remain up to date and aligned with the current state of the data, which is essential for preserving predictive performance.

Reproducibility is another major benefit of automated workflows. By encoding every step of the data and model pipeline in code, teams can ensure that results are consistent and auditable. This is particularly important in regulated industries, where transparency and traceability are mandatory. Version control systems like Git, combined with environment management tools such as Docker or Conda, make it possible to capture the exact state of the pipeline at any given point in time. This facilitates collaboration across teams, simplifies debugging, and accelerates onboarding for new team members.

Scalability is also enhanced through automated pipelines. As data volumes grow, pipelines must be able to handle increased load without significant degradation in performance. Distributed processing frameworks such as Apache Spark, Dask, or Flink allow for parallel execution of tasks across multiple nodes, significantly reducing processing time for large datasets. Integration with cloud platforms provides elasticity, allowing pipelines to scale resources up or down based on workload demands. Cloud-native orchestration tools such as Google Cloud Composer, AWS Step Functions, or Azure Data Factory offer additional capabilities tailored for enterprise-scale deployments.

Security and data governance are integral to automated workflows. Pipelines must enforce access controls, encrypt data in transit and at rest, and log all data handling activities. Sensitive data must be handled in accordance with compliance requirements such as GDPR, HIPAA, or CCPA. Workflow automation tools often include features for managing credentials, masking data, and auditing user actions. These measures not only protect data but also build trust among stakeholders and ensure that data handling aligns with organizational policies and legal standards.

Collaboration between data engineers, data scientists, and operations teams is facilitated by clearly defined pipelines and automated workflows. Each team can focus on their area of expertise while relying on the pipeline to integrate their contributions into a cohesive process. Data engineers ensure data quality and performance, data scientists focus on model development and validation, and DevOps teams oversee deployment and infrastructure. This division of labor enhances productivity and accelerates delivery, making it possible to move from experimentation to production more quickly and reliably.

The development of modular and reusable components within a pipeline encourages best practices and code reusability. Instead of rewriting the same logic multiple times, teams can build libraries of tested components that can be composed in different ways depending on the task. This not only reduces duplication but also improves maintainability and reduces the likelihood of errors. Pipelines can be parameterized to support different configurations, datasets, or environments, making them flexible and adaptable to a variety of use cases.

As data becomes more central to strategic decision-making, the importance of robust data pipelines and automated workflows continues to grow. These systems enable organizations to process data efficiently, maintain high-quality standards, and respond quickly to changing business needs. They reduce the burden of manual intervention, minimize errors, and create a foundation for scalable and sustainable data science practices. With the right tools and practices, teams can build pipelines that are not only powerful and efficient but also transparent, secure, and easy to manage. Mastery of data pipeline design and workflow automation is thus a critical skill for modern data professionals, forming the backbone of effective data infrastructure and intelligent decision systems.

Model Deployment Strategies

Model deployment is the phase in the machine learning lifecycle where trained models are moved from development environments into production systems so they can generate predictions in real-time or on a scheduled basis. While building and training models can be complex, deploying them introduces an entirely different set of challenges. These include ensuring scalability, reliability, security, and maintainability. The strategy used to deploy a model depends on the specific use case, infrastructure, and organizational requirements. A robust deployment strategy ensures that models deliver value in practical settings, supporting business operations or enhancing user experiences with minimal disruption and maximum efficiency.

The first consideration in deployment is the type of model serving required. Batch inference and real-time inference are two primary modes. Batch inference involves generating predictions for large volumes of data at once, typically scheduled during off-peak hours. This is common in use cases like generating customer scores, forecasting demand, or updating recommendations overnight. Real-time inference, on the other hand, requires the model to respond instantly to incoming data, such as in fraud detection systems, chatbots, or personalized search engines. The infrastructure for real-time serving needs to be optimized for low latency, high availability, and efficient resource utilization.

Containerization has emerged as a key enabler of model deployment. By packaging models along with their dependencies and runtime environments into containers, such as Docker images, teams can ensure consistent behavior across different environments. This encapsulation simplifies the deployment process and allows models to be moved easily between development, testing, and production stages. Containers also enable horizontal scaling, where multiple instances of the model can be run in parallel to handle increased load. Container orchestration platforms like Kubernetes automate the management of containerized applications, providing tools for scaling, monitoring, and maintaining uptime.

RESTful APIs are a common method for exposing machine learning models as services. By wrapping the model in a web framework, such as Flask or FastAPI, developers can create endpoints that accept input data and return predictions. These APIs can then be integrated into larger applications, allowing other systems to interact with the model seamlessly. This architecture supports both real-time and asynchronous workflows and makes it easier to log requests, apply rate limiting, and enforce authentication. For more advanced scenarios, gRPC may be used as an alternative to REST for high-performance communication between services.

Model versioning is an essential practice in deployment. Each iteration of a model may involve different training data, features, or hyperparameters, and keeping track of these versions ensures that updates can be audited, compared, or rolled back if necessary. Tools like MLflow, DVC, and ModelDB provide solutions for tracking model versions, including metadata, metrics, and code artifacts. When deploying new versions, organizations must decide how to introduce them without disrupting the user experience or business processes. This is where deployment strategies such as blue-green deployments and canary releases come into play.

Blue-green deployment involves maintaining two identical environments—one for the current production model (blue) and one for the new version (green). Once the new model is tested and deemed ready, traffic is switched from the blue environment to the green environment. This approach allows for quick rollback in case of failure and minimizes downtime. Canary deployment takes a more gradual approach, releasing the new model to a small subset of users or traffic while monitoring performance. If the new version performs well, the deployment is expanded incrementally. These strategies reduce risk and allow teams to validate model behavior under real-world conditions before a full rollout.

Monitoring and logging are critical components of a deployment strategy. Once a model is live, it must be continuously observed to ensure that it performs as expected. This includes tracking prediction accuracy, input data drift, latency, error rates, and resource consumption. Model degradation can occur over time due to changes in data distributions or user behavior, a phenomenon known as concept drift. Detecting these changes early allows for timely retraining or adjustments. Tools such as Prometheus, Grafana, and Seldon Core can be integrated into the deployment stack to provide real-time monitoring and visualization.

Security considerations must also be addressed when deploying models. Exposure to external environments introduces risks related to unauthorized access, data leakage, and adversarial attacks. Secure deployment involves implementing encryption in transit and at rest, authenticating API access, validating input data, and restricting model access to trusted services. In sensitive domains like healthcare or finance, additional compliance requirements may apply, necessitating auditing capabilities and detailed logging of model decisions.

Deployment strategies must also consider the environment in which the model will operate. Edge deployment is increasingly important for applications that require low latency, offline access, or data privacy. In this scenario, models are deployed directly to devices such as smartphones, IoT sensors, or autonomous vehicles. These deployments require models to be lightweight and optimized for limited hardware resources. Techniques like quantization, pruning, and model distillation are used to reduce size and improve inference speed without sacrificing performance.

Another emerging trend is serverless deployment, where models are hosted in a cloud environment that automatically manages resource allocation and scaling. Serverless platforms, such as AWS Lambda or Google Cloud Functions, allow developers to focus on functionality without managing infrastructure. This model is cost-effective for workloads with variable or unpredictable demand, as resources are provisioned only when needed. However, cold start latency and execution time limits can be constraints for certain use cases.

In many organizations, model deployment is part of a broader machine learning operations strategy, known as MLOps. This practice integrates data engineering, model development, testing, deployment, and monitoring into a unified and automated pipeline. MLOps enables continuous integration and continuous delivery for machine learning models, reducing the time from experimentation to production and fostering collaboration across teams. By automating repetitive tasks and enforcing best practices, MLOps enhances reliability, scalability, and governance throughout the model lifecycle.

Choosing the right deployment strategy requires a careful balance between performance, reliability, complexity, and business needs. It involves collaboration among data scientists, software engineers, DevOps teams, and stakeholders. A well-structured deployment process not only ensures that machine learning models deliver value consistently but also lays the groundwork for maintaining and improving these models over time. As the role of AI continues to expand across industries, the ability to deploy models effectively and responsibly becomes a defining capability of data-driven organizations.

Using Cloud Services for Data Science

The rise of cloud computing has dramatically transformed the field of data science, offering powerful tools and scalable infrastructure that enable data professionals to build, train, and deploy models more efficiently than ever before. Cloud services eliminate the need for expensive on-premises hardware and allow teams to access virtually unlimited computing resources on demand. This flexibility supports everything from data storage and processing to advanced analytics and machine learning. By leveraging the cloud, organizations can streamline their workflows, reduce time to insight, and foster collaboration across geographically distributed teams.

Cloud platforms such as Amazon Web Services, Microsoft Azure, and Google Cloud Platform provide a comprehensive suite of services tailored for data science. These services include data storage, data integration, distributed computing, machine learning platforms, visualization tools, and model deployment environments. The ability to seamlessly integrate these components within a single ecosystem allows for the construction of end-to-end data science pipelines that are scalable, secure, and easy to maintain. Cloud services also support multiple programming environments, including Python, R, and SQL, ensuring compatibility with a wide range of tools and libraries used in the data science community.

One of the foundational services in the cloud is data storage. Cloud storage options such as Amazon S3, Google Cloud Storage, and Azure Blob Storage offer highly durable, scalable, and cost-effective solutions for storing raw data, intermediate files, and model artifacts. These systems support a variety of data formats and can be accessed through APIs or integrated directly into other cloud-based services. Cloud storage is also critical for maintaining data lakes, which store structured and unstructured data at scale, enabling exploratory analysis and feeding downstream applications such as machine learning models.

Data processing is another crucial aspect of cloud-based data science. Cloud platforms provide services such as AWS Glue, Azure Data Factory, and Google Cloud Dataflow that automate data ingestion, transformation, and loading processes. These services support both batch and real-time processing and can integrate with external data sources such as relational databases, NoSQL systems, and streaming platforms. For large-scale data processing tasks, distributed computing frameworks like Apache Spark, available through managed services such as AWS EMR, Databricks, and Google Cloud Dataproc, provide the computational power needed to analyze terabytes or petabytes of data efficiently.

Cloud services also offer robust environments for building and training machine learning models. Tools like Amazon SageMaker, Azure Machine Learning, and Google Vertex AI provide fully managed platforms that support the entire machine learning lifecycle. These platforms offer built-in algorithms, support for custom model development, automatic model tuning, and experiment tracking. They also provide features for training at scale using GPU and TPU instances, which significantly accelerate the development of deep learning models. Integrated notebooks allow data scientists to develop models interactively, test them quickly, and track their results within the same platform.

Another key benefit of using cloud services for data science is the ability to operationalize models efficiently. Once a model is trained, it can be deployed as a RESTful API, embedded into applications, or scheduled for batch inference. Services such as SageMaker Endpoints, Azure ML Endpoints, and Google AI Platform Prediction make it easy to deploy models with high availability and auto-scaling capabilities. These services support version control, logging, and monitoring, ensuring that deployed models can be managed and updated without service interruptions. The cloud also simplifies the integration of models into business workflows, enabling real-time decision-making and automation of tasks.

Security and compliance are top priorities when working with sensitive data in the cloud. Cloud providers offer extensive security features, including data encryption at rest and in transit, role-based access control, identity management, and auditing capabilities. These features ensure that data is protected from unauthorized access and that compliance with industry regulations such as GDPR, HIPAA, and SOC 2 is maintained. In addition to native security tools, third-party solutions can be integrated to enhance monitoring, anomaly detection, and incident response capabilities.

Collaboration is greatly enhanced through cloud services. Teams can share datasets, code, and models in a centralized environment, enabling seamless communication and faster iteration. Cloud-hosted version control systems such as GitHub and GitLab, often integrated into development environments, support collaborative coding and model versioning. Shared notebooks, dashboards, and reports allow data scientists, analysts, and business stakeholders to explore data and insights together in real time. This shared infrastructure reduces duplication of effort and promotes transparency in data science workflows.

Cloud-based services also support automation and orchestration of data science tasks. Workflow tools like Apache Airflow, Azure Data Factory pipelines, and Google Cloud Composer allow users to schedule and monitor complex workflows that span multiple services. These tools support dependency management, error handling, and alerting, making it easier to maintain reliable and reproducible pipelines. Automation enables continuous integration and delivery in machine learning, where models can be retrained, validated, and redeployed based on new data or changing conditions.

The elasticity of cloud services ensures that resources can be scaled up or down based on demand. During peak times, additional compute instances can be provisioned automatically to handle increased workloads. Conversely, resources can be deallocated during periods of low activity to reduce costs. This pay-as-you-go model allows organizations to optimize resource usage and budget more effectively. Reserved and spot instances offer further cost-saving opportunities by allowing users to choose pricing models that match their workload requirements.

Cloud marketplaces offer access to prebuilt datasets, APIs, machine learning models, and software tools that accelerate development. These resources can be integrated into projects with minimal configuration, providing a head start for common tasks such as image recognition, natural language processing, and anomaly detection. Cloud platforms also support hybrid and multi-cloud strategies, enabling organizations to leverage the strengths of different providers and ensure redundancy and business continuity.

Using cloud services for data science empowers organizations to innovate faster, scale seamlessly, and adapt quickly to changing demands. It reduces the barriers to entry for small teams by providing access to enterprise-grade infrastructure and tools, while also supporting the needs of large organizations with complex data ecosystems. As the demand for data-driven insights continues to grow, the ability to harness cloud technologies effectively becomes a key differentiator. Mastery of cloud platforms not only enhances the capabilities of individual data scientists but also transforms how entire organizations approach analytics, experimentation, and decision-making in a digital world.

Introduction to MLOps

Machine Learning Operations, commonly referred to as MLOps, is a discipline that combines machine learning, DevOps, and data engineering to streamline and automate the deployment, monitoring, and governance of machine learning models in production environments. As organizations increasingly adopt machine learning to power critical applications, the need to operationalize models and ensure their consistent performance, scalability, and reliability has grown significantly. MLOps addresses these needs by applying best practices from software engineering to the machine learning lifecycle, enabling teams to manage models in a robust, scalable, and repeatable manner.

Traditional machine learning workflows often focus heavily on the experimentation phase, where data scientists build and evaluate models using historical datasets. However, once a model has been trained and validated, the challenge lies in deploying it into production systems where it must make real-time decisions, interact with users or other systems, and adapt to changing data conditions. Without a structured operational framework, deploying models can become a slow, error-prone process that hampers innovation and increases technical debt. MLOps provides the tools, processes, and culture necessary to bridge the gap between development and production, ensuring that models deliver value continuously and reliably.

A fundamental component of MLOps is automation. Automated pipelines are designed to handle tasks such as data preprocessing, model training, hyperparameter tuning, evaluation, deployment, and monitoring. These pipelines reduce manual intervention and minimize inconsistencies that arise from ad hoc processes. For example, a well-defined training pipeline can automatically fetch the latest data, apply transformations, retrain the model, validate its performance, and package it for deployment. This not only accelerates the development cycle but also ensures reproducibility and traceability, as every step is codified and logged.

Version control is another key aspect of MLOps. Just as software developers use tools like Git to manage code changes, MLOps extends versioning to include datasets, model parameters, training scripts, and configuration files. This comprehensive versioning enables teams to reproduce experiments, track model lineage, and compare different versions based on performance metrics. Tools such as DVC (Data Version Control), MLflow, and Weights & Biases help manage this complexity by integrating versioning, tracking, and collaboration into the machine learning workflow.

Continuous integration and continuous delivery, or CI/CD, are central practices in MLOps. CI ensures that changes to code, data, or models are automatically tested and validated in isolated environments before they are merged into the main pipeline. This helps catch bugs early and enforces consistency across environments. CD automates the process of deploying validated models to production, reducing the time and effort required to move from experimentation to real-world application. Together, CI/CD pipelines promote agility and reliability, enabling rapid iteration while maintaining high quality standards.

Monitoring and observability are crucial for maintaining the health of machine learning models in production. Once deployed, models are exposed to live data, which may differ significantly from the data used during training. Data drift, concept drift, and changes in user behavior can degrade model performance over time. MLOps emphasizes the need for continuous monitoring of key metrics such as prediction accuracy, latency, input distribution, and resource usage. By setting up alerts and dashboards, teams can detect anomalies early, trigger automated retraining, or roll back to previous model versions when necessary.

Model governance is another important pillar of MLOps. It involves establishing policies and controls to ensure that models are developed, deployed, and used responsibly. This includes maintaining documentation, validating ethical considerations, securing data privacy, and complying with industry regulations. In regulated sectors such as finance and healthcare, governance requirements are stringent, and MLOps practices provide the necessary infrastructure to support audit trails, access controls, and model explainability. By embedding governance into the machine learning lifecycle, organizations can reduce risk and foster trust in automated decision systems.

Collaboration is enhanced through MLOps by enabling seamless interaction between data scientists, machine learning engineers, DevOps teams, and business stakeholders. MLOps platforms provide shared workspaces, experiment tracking, and reproducible environments, allowing teams to work in parallel while maintaining alignment. Clear interfaces and modular pipelines facilitate handoffs between roles and reduce dependencies that can slow down development. This collaborative environment fosters innovation and ensures that models are aligned with business objectives throughout their lifecycle.

Scalability is a core advantage of MLOps practices. As the volume of data and the number of models increase, managing infrastructure manually becomes infeasible. MLOps platforms support dynamic scaling of compute resources, enabling efficient handling of large datasets and model training jobs. Cloud-native tools such as Kubernetes, Kubeflow, and SageMaker Pipelines provide the foundation for scalable MLOps, allowing teams to deploy models across distributed environments with resilience and flexibility. These tools also support the deployment of models to various endpoints, including edge devices, web services, and batch processing systems.

Testing in MLOps extends beyond traditional unit and integration tests. Models must be evaluated for fairness, bias, robustness, and explainability. Automated test suites can include checks for data quality, feature distribution, and model behavior under adversarial inputs. This ensures that models meet not only functional requirements but also ethical and operational standards. Incorporating these tests into the CI/CD pipeline allows for early detection of issues and reduces the risk of deploying flawed models.

MLOps is not a one-size-fits-all solution but rather a set of principles and practices that can be adapted to different organizational needs and maturity levels. For startups, it may begin with automating a few steps in the pipeline, such as model training and deployment. For large enterprises, it may involve fully integrated platforms that support hundreds of models and petabytes of data. Regardless of scale, the goal is to bring discipline, consistency, and scalability to machine learning operations.

As machine learning becomes more deeply embedded in products and services, the demand for robust operational practices will only grow. MLOps empowers organizations to deliver reliable and responsible AI at scale. It transforms machine learning from a laboratory activity into a repeatable, scalable, and governed engineering process. By investing in MLOps, organizations can accelerate innovation, reduce technical debt, and ensure that their models continue to deliver value long after they are deployed. The adoption of MLOps marks a critical evolution in the way data science is practiced, bringing it into alignment with the rigor and reliability expected in modern software engineering.

Ethical Considerations in Data Science

As data science continues to reshape industries, influence decisions, and power artificial intelligence systems, the ethical implications of its practices have gained increasing attention. The powerful tools and algorithms developed by data scientists can have significant social, economic, and political consequences. These tools are often deployed in domains like healthcare, finance, education, law enforcement, and social media, where the outcomes affect individuals and communities. Therefore, ethical considerations must be an integral part of the entire data science lifecycle, from data collection and preprocessing to model deployment and monitoring. Ignoring these ethical dimensions can lead to biased systems, discrimination, privacy violations, and a general erosion of public trust.

One of the most prominent ethical concerns in data science is bias and fairness. Algorithms trained on historical data can perpetuate or even amplify existing societal biases if those biases are reflected in the data. For example, a recruitment algorithm trained on past hiring data may learn to favor certain demographics over others if historical hiring practices were discriminatory. In lending, models may deny credit to individuals from specific communities if the training data reflects systemic economic disparities. These outcomes are not just statistical artifacts; they have real-world implications that can marginalize vulnerable populations and reinforce inequality. Addressing algorithmic bias requires careful examination of data sources, consideration of the social context, and implementation of fairness-aware learning techniques.

Fairness in data science is complex and context-dependent. There is no single universal definition of fairness, and different situations may call for different fairness criteria, such as equal opportunity, demographic parity, or individual fairness. Choosing an appropriate fairness metric often involves trade-offs and value judgments. Moreover, achieving fairness may require interventions that go beyond technical adjustments, such as engaging with stakeholders, revisiting institutional policies, or questioning the underlying objectives of the analysis. Ethical data science thus requires a multidisciplinary approach that incorporates perspectives from law, sociology, philosophy, and human rights.

Another critical ethical issue is privacy. The ability of data scientists to collect, store, and analyze vast amounts of personal information raises concerns about how that data is used and protected. Users may not always be aware of how their data is collected, what it is used for, or who has access to it. In some cases, data may be used in ways that individuals did not consent to or anticipate. Even anonymized datasets can sometimes be re-identified by combining them with other data sources, exposing individuals to risks they did not agree to take. Ethical data practices must ensure transparency, obtain informed consent, and apply robust data protection techniques such as encryption, differential privacy, and secure multi-party computation.

The principle of transparency also extends to the models themselves. Many machine learning algorithms, particularly complex models like deep neural networks, are considered black boxes because their internal logic is difficult to interpret. This lack of explainability can be problematic when the model's outputs impact decisions such as hiring, insurance rates, parole eligibility, or medical treatment. People affected by such decisions have the right to understand how they were made. Model interpretability is therefore not just a technical challenge but also a matter of accountability and trust. Techniques like feature importance scores, surrogate models, and local explanation methods are being developed to help make models more transparent, but these methods must be used with care and an understanding of their limitations.

In addition to fairness, privacy, and transparency, data science also raises ethical questions about responsibility and accountability. When a machine learning system causes harm, it is not always clear who is to blame. Is it the data scientist who developed the model, the engineer who deployed it, the organization that funded it, or the user who acted on its predictions? Establishing clear lines of accountability is essential for ethical governance. Organizations must adopt ethical guidelines and governance structures that define roles, responsibilities, and escalation procedures in case of harm. These structures should also include mechanisms for redress, allowing individuals to appeal decisions and seek corrections when they believe they have been wronged.

Furthermore, ethical data science demands attention to the broader impacts of technology on society. Automation powered by data science can displace jobs, reshape labor markets, and influence social behavior. Recommendation algorithms can amplify misinformation, polarize public discourse, or manipulate user behavior for profit. Predictive policing systems can reinforce surveillance in already over-policed communities, creating feedback loops that exacerbate injustice. These impacts are not merely side effects; they are shaped by the design choices, incentives, and values embedded in the technology. Data scientists must critically assess the potential societal consequences of their work and strive to design systems that promote equity, justice, and public good.

Ethical challenges also emerge in the global context. Data science projects deployed across countries must respect cultural differences, legal frameworks, and local norms. Practices that are considered acceptable in one region may be unethical or illegal in another. Cross-border data transfers, for instance, may violate data sovereignty laws or undermine the rights of individuals in jurisdictions with weaker protections. Moreover, the benefits of data science are often unevenly distributed, with high-income countries reaping disproportionate advantages from global data flows. Ethical data science must be globally conscious, inclusive, and committed to equitable development.

To foster ethical practices in data science, education and awareness are essential. Ethical reasoning should be a core part of data science curricula, alongside technical skills. Practitioners must be trained to recognize ethical dilemmas, engage in critical thinking, and collaborate with stakeholders to make informed decisions. Organizations must cultivate ethical cultures that encourage questioning, reflection, and accountability. Ethical review boards, impact assessments, and continuous monitoring can help institutionalize ethical standards and guide responsible innovation.

Ultimately, ethical considerations in data science are about aligning technological capabilities with human values. They challenge data scientists to look beyond accuracy and efficiency and to consider the dignity, rights, and well-being of the people affected by their work. This requires humility, empathy, and a commitment to using data and algorithms not just to optimize outcomes but to improve lives. In a world increasingly shaped by data, ethical vigilance is not optional but fundamental to the integrity and legitimacy of the data science profession.

Bias and Fairness in Machine Learning

Bias and fairness in machine learning have become critical areas of concern as algorithms increasingly influence decisions that affect people's lives. From credit scoring and hiring to healthcare and criminal justice, automated systems are now embedded in domains with serious social and ethical implications. When machine learning models are trained on historical data, they can inadvertently learn and perpetuate existing biases, leading to outcomes that unfairly disadvantage certain individuals or groups. Understanding how bias enters machine learning systems and how fairness can be defined and enforced is essential for building responsible and equitable technology.

Bias in machine learning can originate from multiple sources. One of the most common sources is biased training data. Historical datasets may reflect existing societal inequalities, discriminatory practices, or unbalanced representation. If an employment dataset reflects past preferences for male candidates, a model trained on this data may replicate the same preference and systematically disadvantage women. Similarly, if crime data is disproportionately collected from certain neighborhoods due to over-policing, models trained on this data may associate higher risk with these areas, regardless of individual behavior. These issues are compounded by the fact that many machine learning algorithms are optimized for overall accuracy without regard for how errors are distributed across different groups.

Another source of bias is data labeling. Supervised learning models depend on labeled data, which often involves human judgment. If the labeling process is subjective or inconsistent, the model can learn from and amplify these inconsistencies. For example, in medical diagnostics, if doctors tend to underdiagnose certain conditions in specific demographic groups, those patterns may be encoded into the model, leading to underdiagnosis in future predictions. Labeling bias is particularly problematic in areas like content moderation, emotion recognition, or sentiment analysis, where personal opinions and cultural context can heavily influence labels.

Feature selection and representation can also introduce bias. The choice of which variables to include in a model and how they are encoded can have profound implications. Some features may serve as proxies for protected attributes such as race, gender, or socioeconomic status. For instance, using zip code as a feature in a credit scoring model may indirectly encode racial information due to residential segregation. Even when sensitive attributes are removed, correlated variables can reintroduce bias. This phenomenon, known as proxy discrimination, highlights the complexity of eliminating bias solely through feature exclusion.

Bias can also arise during model training and evaluation. Many algorithms make assumptions that may not hold across different groups, leading to disparate performance. For example, a model may achieve high accuracy overall but perform poorly on underrepresented subgroups. If evaluation metrics do not account for this disparity, the model may be deployed without awareness of its differential impact. Fairness-aware evaluation requires disaggregated analysis, where metrics such as precision, recall, and false positive rates are calculated separately for different demographic groups. Only then can disparities be detected and addressed.

Defining fairness in machine learning is challenging because it involves normative judgments and context-dependent trade-offs. Several formal definitions have been proposed, each reflecting different fairness criteria. One common definition is demographic parity, which requires that the outcome of a model is independent of sensitive attributes like race or gender. Another is equal opportunity, which demands that individuals from different groups who qualify for a positive outcome have equal chances of receiving it. Yet another is individual fairness, which asserts that similar individuals should be treated similarly. These definitions are often mathematically incompatible, meaning that satisfying one may violate another. The choice of fairness criterion must therefore be informed by the context of the application, stakeholder values, and the potential consequences of different types of errors.

Mitigating bias in machine learning requires a multifaceted approach. Preprocessing techniques aim to remove bias from the data before training. This can involve resampling, reweighting, or transforming the data to balance representation or equalize distributions across groups. In-processing methods modify the learning algorithm itself to incorporate fairness constraints during training. This can include adding regularization terms to penalize disparate impact or designing algorithms that optimize for fairness metrics alongside accuracy. Post-processing approaches adjust the model's outputs to achieve fairness, such as by equalizing decision thresholds across groups or calibrating probabilities. Each method has its advantages and limitations, and often a combination of techniques is necessary to achieve satisfactory results.

Transparency and accountability are essential for addressing bias and promoting fairness. Organizations must be able to explain how their models work, what data was used, and how fairness was assessed. Documentation practices such as model cards and data sheets help provide context, assumptions, and limitations of models and datasets. External audits, impact assessments, and community engagement can further enhance accountability and trust. These practices not only help identify and mitigate bias but also foster dialogue about the ethical implications of machine learning applications.

Bias mitigation is not a one-time effort but an ongoing process. Data distributions can shift over time, leading to changes in model behavior and potential reintroduction of bias. Continuous monitoring and feedback loops are necessary to ensure that models remain fair and effective in dynamic environments. This includes tracking fairness metrics over time, conducting regular retraining, and updating models in response to changing data or social conditions. Stakeholder involvement throughout the lifecycle of a machine learning system—

from design to deployment to monitoring—is crucial for maintaining alignment with fairness goals.

Ultimately, the challenge of bias and fairness in machine learning is not just a technical one but also a social and ethical one. It requires recognizing that algorithms do not exist in a vacuum but reflect the values and structures of the societies in which they are embedded. Data scientists, engineers, and decision-makers must therefore approach their work with a commitment to inclusivity, responsibility, and justice. By integrating fairness into the design, evaluation, and governance of machine learning systems, it is possible to build technologies that serve all members of society more equitably. The pursuit of fairness must be an integral part of the data science profession, guiding how problems are framed, solutions are developed, and outcomes are assessed. Only then can machine learning fulfill its promise as a tool for positive social impact.

Interpreting Machine Learning Models

As machine learning becomes increasingly integrated into decision-making systems across industries, the ability to interpret and understand model behavior has become a critical requirement. Interpretation refers to the process of explaining the internal mechanisms and decision logic of a model in a way that is understandable to humans. While traditional statistical models like linear regression are inherently interpretable due to their simplicity, modern machine learning algorithms such as ensemble models and deep neural networks are often referred to as black boxes because of their complexity and lack of transparency. Interpreting these models is essential not only for building trust with users but also for ensuring accountability, improving model performance, diagnosing issues, and meeting regulatory requirements.

Interpretability is particularly important in high-stakes domains such as healthcare, finance, criminal justice, and education, where automated decisions can significantly impact individuals' lives. In these settings, it is not sufficient for a model to simply perform well according to quantitative metrics. Stakeholders, including regulators, subject matter experts, and end-users, often need to understand how and why a particular prediction was made. This understanding can inform better decision-making, help identify and mitigate bias, and support transparency and ethical use of machine learning.

There are two primary approaches to interpreting machine learning models: intrinsic interpretability and post hoc interpretability. Intrinsically interpretable models are those whose structures and parameters are easy to understand by design. Examples include decision trees, linear models, and rule-based systems. These models allow users to trace decision paths, examine feature coefficients, and understand the effect of each input on the output. However, these models may not capture complex patterns in the data as effectively as more sophisticated algorithms, which often leads to a trade-off between accuracy and interpretability.

Post hoc interpretability, on the other hand, refers to techniques that are applied after a model has been trained, regardless of its complexity, to extract explanations about its predictions. These techniques can be either model-specific or model-agnostic. Model-specific methods are tailored to particular classes of models, such as gradient boosting machines or neural networks, and often provide more accurate explanations. Model-agnostic methods, in contrast, can be applied to any model and are therefore more flexible. One widely used model-agnostic technique is permutation importance, which measures the impact of each feature on model performance by randomly shuffling its values and observing the change in the prediction error.

Another popular interpretability method is Partial Dependence Plots, which illustrate the marginal effect of a feature on the predicted outcome by averaging out the influence of other features. This technique helps visualize how changes in a specific variable affect the model's predictions, offering insights into the relationships captured by the model. However, partial dependence plots assume feature independence and can be misleading when features are highly correlated. To address this limitation, Accumulated Local Effects plots have been introduced, which decompose the model's output more reliably in the presence of correlated features.

Local interpretability methods focus on explaining individual predictions rather than the model as a whole. One such method is LIME, or Local Interpretable Model-agnostic Explanations. LIME approximates the model locally around a specific prediction by fitting a simpler, interpretable model, such as linear regression, using perturbed samples of the input data. This local surrogate model helps identify which features contributed most to the prediction. Another powerful local interpretation tool is SHAP, or SHapley Additive exPlanations. SHAP values are based on game theory and attribute the contribution of each feature by calculating the average marginal effect across all possible feature combinations. SHAP values are consistent and additive, providing a unified measure of feature importance that can be aggregated across predictions to gain global insights.

In addition to these technical methods, visualization plays a key role in interpretability. Heatmaps, saliency maps, and attention maps are commonly used to explain the behavior of image and text models. For example, in computer vision tasks, saliency maps highlight the regions of an image that were most influential in the model's decision. In natural language processing, attention mechanisms show which words the model focused on when generating a prediction, offering intuitive insights into how context and language structure affect the outcome.

Despite the availability of these interpretability tools, challenges remain. Interpretability is inherently subjective and depends on the audience. What is interpretable to a data scientist may not be interpretable to a clinician or a policy maker. Effective communication of model explanations requires understanding the needs, expectations, and background knowledge of the target audience. This may involve simplifying technical language, using analogies, or providing interactive interfaces that allow users to explore model behavior dynamically. Interpretability must also strike a balance with performance, complexity, and privacy, as overly detailed explanations may expose sensitive information or lead to gaming of the model.

Interpretability is also closely related to model debugging and improvement. By understanding which features influence predictions and how, data scientists can identify issues such as data leakage, model overfitting, or underutilized features. This understanding can guide feature engineering, model selection, and hyperparameter tuning. It also supports the validation of domain knowledge, helping ensure that the model aligns with real-world expectations and constraints. Interpretability can serve as a feedback mechanism for continuous model refinement and quality assurance.

In regulated industries, interpretability is often mandated by law or industry standards. For example, the European Union's General Data Protection Regulation includes a right to explanation, which entitles individuals to meaningful information about automated decisions affecting them. Meeting such requirements demands more than just technical tools; it requires establishing governance frameworks, documentation practices, and audit trails that support transparency and accountability throughout the model lifecycle. Interpretability thus becomes a foundational component of ethical and responsible AI.

As machine learning systems become more pervasive, interpretability will continue to evolve as a field of research and practice. Advances in human-centered design, interactive machine learning, and causal inference promise to make explanations more meaningful, actionable, and aligned with human reasoning. Interpreting machine learning models is not merely a technical challenge but a social and ethical one, requiring collaboration between data scientists, domain experts, and affected communities. By making models more understandable, we empower people to trust, question, and engage with the systems that increasingly shape our lives. Interpretability is not an optional add-on but a core requirement for the responsible and effective deployment of machine learning.

Data Science in Healthcare

The integration of data science into healthcare has led to transformative advancements in how medical information is collected, analyzed, and applied to improve patient outcomes and streamline operations. With the digitization of health records, the proliferation of wearable devices, and the growing availability of medical imaging and genomic data, healthcare systems now generate massive volumes of diverse data. Data science provides the tools and techniques needed to process this complex information and derive meaningful insights that can drive clinical decision-making, operational efficiency, personalized treatment, and disease prevention. The application of data science in healthcare is not merely a technological shift; it represents a fundamental evolution in the way medicine is practiced and delivered.

One of the most impactful areas of data science in healthcare is predictive analytics. By using historical data from electronic health records, insurance claims, and patient demographics, predictive models can identify individuals at risk for developing chronic diseases such as diabetes, heart failure, or cancer. These models analyze patterns in the data to forecast future outcomes and enable proactive interventions. For instance, a patient with a history of high blood pressure and elevated cholesterol levels may be flagged as high risk for a cardiac event, prompting closer monitoring or lifestyle interventions. Predictive analytics also supports hospital management by forecasting patient admissions, readmission risks, and emergency room visits, which allows for better resource allocation and staffing.

Machine learning, a core component of data science, plays a pivotal role in enhancing diagnostic accuracy. Algorithms trained on large datasets of medical images can detect abnormalities in radiology scans such as X-rays, MRIs, and CT scans with a level of precision that rivals or even exceeds that of human experts. These systems assist radiologists in identifying tumors, fractures, and other conditions, improving diagnostic speed and reducing errors. In pathology, machine learning models analyze tissue samples to detect signs of disease at a cellular level, aiding in the early detection of cancer and other serious illnesses. By combining image analysis with patient history and clinical data, diagnostic tools can offer more comprehensive assessments.

Natural language processing is another key area where data science is making significant contributions to healthcare. Much of the valuable information in healthcare is stored in unstructured text, such as clinical notes, discharge summaries, and pathology reports. NLP techniques extract and structure this information, enabling more effective analysis and integration with other data sources. For example, NLP can identify mentions of symptoms, diagnoses, medications, and treatment plans from clinical narratives, providing a richer understanding of a patient's health status. This capability enhances clinical decision support systems, which offer real-time recommendations to clinicians based on current evidence and individual patient data.

Personalized medicine is an emerging field that relies heavily on data science to tailor treatments to individual patients based on genetic, environmental, and lifestyle factors. By analyzing genomic data, data scientists can uncover genetic markers associated with particular diseases or drug responses. This information enables the development of targeted therapies that are more effective and have fewer side effects. In oncology, for example, genomic profiling of tumors allows for the selection of therapies that are most likely to be effective against specific cancer mutations. Personalized medicine not only improves treatment outcomes but also reduces the trial-and-error approach often associated with conventional treatment strategies.

Operational efficiency in healthcare delivery is another area where data science has made substantial inroads. Hospitals and clinics use data analytics to optimize scheduling, reduce wait times, and manage supply chains. Predictive models forecast demand for services, helping facilities prepare for surges in patient volume, such as during flu season or pandemics. By analyzing patterns in workflow and patient throughput, healthcare administrators can identify bottlenecks and implement process improvements. Data-driven decision-making leads to better utilization of resources, cost savings, and enhanced patient satisfaction.

Population health management benefits greatly from the insights provided by data science. By aggregating and analyzing data across populations, healthcare providers can identify public health trends, track the spread of infectious diseases, and evaluate the effectiveness of interventions. During the COVID-19 pandemic, data science was instrumental in modeling the spread of the virus, predicting hospital capacity needs, and informing public health policies. Surveillance systems that integrate data from multiple sources provide early warnings of outbreaks, enabling timely responses. Data science also supports health equity initiatives by identifying disparities in access to care, treatment outcomes, and health behaviors among different demographic groups.

Clinical trials and biomedical research are increasingly driven by data science methodologies. Advanced analytics help design more efficient trials, identify suitable participants, and monitor safety and efficacy in real time. Data science accelerates the discovery of new drugs and treatments by mining large biomedical databases and applying machine learning to identify promising compounds or therapeutic targets. The integration of multi-omics data, including genomics, proteomics, and metabolomics, provides a comprehensive view of disease mechanisms and supports the development of precision therapies. Research institutions and pharmaceutical companies leverage these capabilities to shorten the drug development timeline and reduce costs.

Despite its many benefits, the application of data science in healthcare also raises important ethical and regulatory considerations. Patient privacy is paramount, and the handling of sensitive health data must comply with regulations such as HIPAA and GDPR. Ensuring data security, informed consent, and transparency in algorithmic decision-making is essential for maintaining trust. Bias in data or algorithms can lead to disparities in treatment or outcomes, making it critical to audit models regularly and incorporate fairness measures. Collaboration between data scientists, clinicians, ethicists, and patients is necessary to navigate these challenges and ensure that innovations serve the best interests of all stakeholders.

Education and training are essential for integrating data science into healthcare effectively. Clinicians need to understand how to interpret and apply data-driven insights, while data scientists must develop a deep understanding of medical contexts and clinical workflows. Interdisciplinary teams that combine expertise in medicine, computer science, and statistics are key to designing systems that are both technically robust and clinically relevant. As the field evolves, continuous learning and collaboration will be vital for keeping pace with new technologies and ensuring that data science continues to contribute positively to health and well-being.

Data science has already begun to reshape healthcare in profound ways, enabling earlier diagnoses, more effective treatments, and better outcomes for patients. Its potential continues to grow as more data becomes available and analytical tools become more sophisticated. The successful integration of data science into healthcare requires not only technical innovation but also a thoughtful approach to ethics, policy, and human-centered design. By harnessing the power of data responsibly and collaboratively, healthcare can become more predictive, preventive, personalized, and participatory, ultimately improving lives on a global scale.

Data Science in Finance

Data science has become an indispensable part of the financial industry, transforming how financial institutions operate, assess risk, detect fraud, and serve their customers. In a domain historically driven by quantitative analysis, the introduction of large-scale data processing and machine learning has opened up new avenues for insight, automation, and decision-making. As financial transactions increasingly occur through digital channels and generate vast amounts of data, data science enables firms to harness this information in ways that provide a competitive advantage, reduce operational costs, and enhance regulatory compliance. The fusion of finance and data science has created a more agile, data-driven financial ecosystem capable of adapting quickly to dynamic market conditions.

One of the most prominent applications of data science in finance is algorithmic trading. Also known as automated or high-frequency trading, this involves the use of complex algorithms that analyze market data, identify trends, and execute trades at speeds and volumes impossible for human traders. These algorithms can process real-time streaming data, news feeds, historical prices, and even social media sentiment to make split-second decisions. Machine learning models learn from past market behavior to predict price movements and optimize trading strategies. By using predictive models, traders can anticipate fluctuations, reduce risk exposure, and capitalize on arbitrage opportunities across markets. Data science also supports the backtesting of trading strategies, allowing firms to simulate their performance under various historical conditions before deploying them in live environments.

Risk management is another area where data science plays a pivotal role. Financial institutions face numerous types of risks, including credit risk, market risk, liquidity risk, and operational risk. Advanced data analytics help quantify these risks more accurately and monitor them in real-time. In credit risk analysis, machine learning models evaluate a borrower's likelihood of default by analyzing a wide range of data points such as payment history, income, employment status, spending behavior, and even alternative data sources like mobile phone usage or social media activity. These models outperform traditional credit scoring systems by capturing complex patterns and nonlinear relationships. For market risk, data science enables stress testing and scenario analysis, helping firms understand how their portfolios would respond to economic shocks, regulatory changes, or geopolitical events.

Fraud detection has been significantly enhanced through the use of data science. Financial fraud is constantly evolving, requiring systems that can detect anomalies and adapt to new threats. Machine learning models are trained on historical transaction data to identify patterns associated with fraudulent activity, such as unusual spending patterns, login behavior, or geographical inconsistencies. These models continuously learn from new data and improve their ability to distinguish between legitimate and suspicious transactions. Real-time fraud detection systems can flag transactions for further review, preventing financial loss and protecting customers. Natural language processing is also used to monitor communications and detect potential misconduct or insider trading in emails, chat logs, and recorded phone calls, which is especially useful for regulatory compliance in investment banking.

Customer analytics is another important application of data science in finance. Banks, insurers, and asset managers use data science to gain a deeper understanding of customer behavior, preferences, and needs. This allows for the development of personalized financial products, tailored marketing campaigns, and improved customer experiences. For instance, recommendation systems suggest relevant banking products, investment opportunities, or insurance plans based on an individual's financial profile. Customer segmentation, enabled by clustering algorithms, helps institutions target specific demographic groups more effectively. Sentiment analysis, powered by natural language processing, evaluates customer feedback and social media activity to gauge satisfaction and anticipate churn. These insights help build stronger relationships with clients and enhance loyalty in a competitive market.

Regulatory compliance and reporting have also benefited from data science innovations. Financial institutions must comply with a wide range of regulations such as anti-money laundering laws, know-your-customer requirements, and financial reporting standards. Data science tools automate the collection, verification, and analysis of regulatory data, reducing manual effort and increasing accuracy. Compliance systems use machine learning to flag suspicious transactions, identify shell companies, and detect complex networks involved in illicit activity. In addition, data science supports real-time reporting and auditing, which enables regulators and firms to monitor compliance more proactively and respond quickly to potential violations. As regulatory frameworks evolve, the flexibility and scalability of data-driven systems ensure that firms can adapt without significant overhauls.

Portfolio management is increasingly being driven by data science, especially in the context of robo-advisors and automated investment platforms. These systems use machine learning algorithms to assess an investor's risk tolerance, financial goals, and market conditions to construct and manage investment portfolios. They continuously monitor performance and rebalance assets as needed to maintain the desired risk-return profile. Data science also enhances the capabilities of traditional portfolio managers by providing tools for asset valuation, volatility forecasting, and diversification analysis. By integrating structured financial data with alternative data sources, such as satellite imagery or web traffic data, analysts can uncover insights that were previously inaccessible.

The insurance industry, a major component of the financial sector, has also embraced data science to refine underwriting, claims processing, and customer engagement. Predictive models assess the likelihood of policyholders filing claims, enabling more accurate pricing and risk stratification. Image recognition and NLP are used to expedite claims assessment and detect fraudulent submissions. Telematics data from connected vehicles informs personalized auto insurance policies based on driving behavior. These data-driven innovations improve efficiency, reduce fraud, and allow insurers to offer more competitive products.

As the reliance on data science grows, ethical considerations and data governance become increasingly important in finance. Decisions driven by algorithms must be transparent and explainable, especially in areas like loan approvals or fraud investigation where outcomes have significant personal and legal implications. Data scientists must ensure that their models do not propagate biases or discriminate against certain populations. Financial institutions are tasked with securing sensitive personal and financial data, requiring robust cybersecurity measures and compliance with data privacy laws such as GDPR. Establishing clear policies for data usage, consent, and accountability is crucial for maintaining trust in a data-driven financial system.

The intersection of finance and data science is one of constant innovation. As new technologies emerge, such as blockchain, quantum computing, and decentralized finance platforms, the role of data science will continue to evolve. The demand for skilled professionals who understand both data science techniques and financial principles is growing rapidly. Organizations must invest in talent development, infrastructure, and cross-functional collaboration to stay ahead in this rapidly changing landscape. The continued integration of data science into finance holds the promise of more efficient markets, better risk management, and improved access to financial services for people around the world. Through responsible use of data and algorithms, the financial industry can become more transparent, inclusive, and responsive to the needs of its customers and stakeholders.

Data Science in Marketing

Data science has revolutionized the field of marketing by turning what was once largely intuition-driven into a highly analytical and data-centric discipline. In a digital economy where customer interactions generate enormous amounts of data every second, marketers are now equipped with the tools to better understand consumer behavior, personalize messaging, optimize campaigns, and measure impact with unprecedented accuracy. By leveraging data science techniques such as predictive analytics, clustering, natural language processing, and machine learning, marketing professionals can develop smarter strategies that improve engagement, reduce costs, and increase return on investment. Data science empowers organizations to create more meaningful connections with their audiences by delivering the right message to the right person at the right time through the right channel.

One of the most powerful applications of data science in marketing is customer segmentation. Rather than relying on broad demographic categories, marketers can use clustering algorithms to divide their customer base into distinct segments based on behavioral, transactional, or psychographic data. These segments may reveal patterns such as high-frequency purchasers, discount-seekers, or first-time buyers. By identifying these unique groups, companies can tailor marketing messages, offers, and product recommendations to suit the specific preferences and needs of each segment. This level of personalization not only enhances the customer experience but also drives higher engagement and conversion rates.

Predictive analytics is another critical tool that helps marketers anticipate future customer behavior. Using historical data, predictive models can forecast outcomes such as the likelihood of a customer making a purchase, churning, or responding to a specific campaign. These insights allow marketing teams to allocate resources more effectively, focus on high-value leads, and proactively address risks. For example, a retailer may use a predictive model to identify customers at risk of lapsing and send them personalized incentives to re-engage. Predictive scoring can also be used to prioritize leads in a sales funnel, ensuring that the sales team focuses their efforts where they are most likely to yield results.

Personalization at scale is one of the hallmarks of data-driven marketing. With the help of recommendation systems, marketers can suggest products, content, or services that align with individual customer preferences. These systems analyze browsing history, purchase patterns, and contextual data to make dynamic recommendations in real time. Streaming platforms use these models to recommend shows or music, while e-commerce websites use them to suggest complementary products or generate personalized homepages. Natural language processing further enhances personalization by enabling chatbots, voice assistants, and sentiment analysis tools to interact with users in a human-like manner and tailor responses based on tone, context, and emotional cues.

Campaign optimization is another area where data science provides significant advantages. A/B testing, uplift modeling, and multi-armed bandit algorithms enable marketers to test different messages, visuals, and delivery times to determine which combinations are most effective. Rather than relying solely on instinct or experience, marketing decisions are grounded in empirical evidence. Data science also allows for real-time campaign adjustments based on performance metrics, ensuring that budgets are allocated to the most successful initiatives. Attribution modeling, which assesses how different touchpoints contribute to a customer's decision to purchase, provides deeper insights into what is working and where improvements are needed. This data-driven approach to optimization improves efficiency and ensures that marketing investments generate measurable results.

Social media analytics is another domain where data science plays a transformative role. Platforms like Twitter, Facebook, and Instagram generate vast amounts of unstructured data in the form of posts, likes, comments, and shares. Data scientists use sentiment analysis, trend detection, and network analysis to understand brand perception, monitor campaign performance, and detect emerging issues in real time. Marketers can track how conversations evolve, identify influential users, and measure the virality of content. This information is invaluable for crafting messaging strategies, responding to crises, and managing reputation. Social listening tools powered by data science help brands stay connected to their audiences and adapt quickly to changing public sentiment.

Customer lifetime value modeling is another key area supported by data science. Understanding the projected future value of a customer relationship enables marketers to make strategic decisions about acquisition and retention. Models that estimate lifetime value take into account factors such as purchase frequency, average order size, and engagement trends. These models help businesses determine how much they can afford to spend to acquire a customer, which customers are worth retaining with special offers, and how to segment customers based on profitability. When combined with predictive churn models, customer lifetime value analysis creates a powerful framework for long-term customer relationship management.

Marketing mix modeling and media planning also benefit from data science. Marketing mix models analyze historical sales and marketing data to quantify the impact of different channels such as TV, radio, digital, and print on overall performance. These models help marketers allocate budgets across channels more effectively, understand seasonality, and identify diminishing returns. Media planning algorithms use historical data, target audience profiles, and campaign goals to create optimal media plans that maximize reach and impact. These insights enable companies to make informed decisions about when, where, and how to invest in advertising for maximum ROI.

Email marketing, one of the most cost-effective digital channels, is enhanced through data science by optimizing send times, subject lines, and content for different segments. Machine learning algorithms can determine the best time to send emails based on user engagement patterns and adapt content based on past interactions. Predictive analytics can forecast open rates and click-through rates, allowing marketers to refine campaigns before they are launched. The ability to track engagement at a granular level also enables personalized follow-ups and nurtures leads more effectively over time.

Data privacy and ethical considerations are becoming increasingly important in marketing as data collection becomes more pervasive. Marketers must ensure that their practices comply with regulations such as GDPR and CCPA, which govern how personal data is collected, stored, and used. Data science plays a role in building privacy-aware systems that anonymize data, limit exposure, and ensure transparency. Ethical marketing also involves being clear with customers about how their data is used and providing them with meaningful choices about consent. Trust is a critical component of brand equity, and responsible data use is essential for maintaining that trust in a data-driven world.

The future of marketing lies in the ability to understand and respond to customer needs in real time, anticipate future behavior, and build lasting relationships through personalized and relevant experiences. Data science provides the foundation for this future by turning raw data into actionable intelligence. As algorithms become more sophisticated and data infrastructure continues to evolve, marketers will be able to deliver even more targeted, efficient, and impactful campaigns. The integration of data science into marketing strategy represents not just a trend, but a fundamental transformation of how businesses engage with their audiences and create value in a highly competitive and connected marketplace.

Real-Time Data Analysis

Real-time data analysis refers to the process of collecting, processing, and analyzing data as it is generated, enabling immediate insights and actions. In a world increasingly driven by instant communication and rapid technological advancement, real-time analysis has become an essential capability across industries. Whether it is monitoring financial markets, managing smart devices in the Internet of Things, providing instantaneous fraud detection, or delivering personalized customer experiences, the ability to interpret data in the moment provides a significant competitive advantage. Traditional data analysis methods that rely on batch processing are insufficient for applications that demand responsiveness, where milliseconds can define success or failure. Real-time data analysis enables organizations to act decisively, detect anomalies as they occur, and dynamically adapt to new information.

The infrastructure for real-time analysis consists of several critical components, including data ingestion, stream processing, storage, and visualization. Data ingestion in real-time scenarios involves continuously capturing data from sources such as sensors, web logs, transactions, user interactions, and social media feeds. This data must be ingested with minimal latency, which requires the use of specialized tools and platforms such as Apache Kafka, Amazon Kinesis, or Google Pub/Sub. These technologies are designed to handle high-throughput, fault-tolerant data streams that allow events to flow in from multiple sources simultaneously.

Once data is ingested, stream processing engines take over to perform transformations, aggregations, and analyses on the fly. Tools such as Apache Flink, Apache Storm, and Apache Spark Streaming are widely used to enable this kind of real-time computation. Unlike batch processing, which waits for all data to be collected before executing computations, stream processing handles data incrementally as it arrives. This means that operations like filtering, joining, and calculating metrics can happen in real time, providing immediate feedback and allowing for responsive system behavior. For instance, a telecommunications provider might monitor network traffic and immediately reroute connections to prevent congestion. In cybersecurity, real-time processing can detect suspicious patterns and trigger alerts before a breach escalates.

Storage of real-time data presents unique challenges due to the volume, velocity, and variability of the data. While some data may be ephemeral and only useful momentarily, other data needs to be persisted for long-term analysis and compliance. Hybrid storage architectures that include both in-memory and persistent storage allow systems to maintain speed while preserving important information. In-memory databases like Redis and Memcached provide rapid access to frequently queried data, while scalable data warehouses like BigQuery, Snowflake, and Redshift store historical data for more comprehensive offline analysis.

Visualization and alerting are essential components of real-time analytics systems, allowing users to interpret data quickly and take appropriate action. Dashboards powered by platforms such as Grafana, Kibana, or Tableau provide dynamic views of streaming data, highlighting key performance indicators, system health metrics, or customer behaviors as they unfold. These dashboards often include automated alerting mechanisms that notify stakeholders when predefined thresholds are crossed or anomalies are detected. This immediacy transforms how decisions are made, shifting from retrospective analysis to proactive management. In operations management, for example, real-time dashboards enable teams to detect production line issues and prevent costly downtime.

Real-time analytics is deeply embedded in modern digital experiences. In e-commerce, it powers dynamic pricing, personalized product recommendations, and real-time inventory updates. By analyzing user clicks, time spent on pages, and purchase patterns in real time, platforms can adjust offers or surface relevant content instantly, enhancing engagement and driving sales. In the financial industry, stock exchanges and trading platforms rely on real-time data to execute transactions, monitor liquidity, and identify market trends. Traders and algorithmic systems make decisions based on live pricing feeds and news data, where even a few milliseconds of delay can result in significant losses or missed opportunities.

In transportation and logistics, real-time data is essential for route optimization, delivery tracking, and fleet management. GPS data, weather conditions, traffic patterns, and delivery statuses are continuously analyzed to improve efficiency and customer satisfaction. Real-time analysis enables predictive maintenance by identifying patterns that signal equipment failure before it happens. By acting on these insights immediately, companies can reduce downtime and extend the lifespan of critical assets. In healthcare, patient monitoring systems track vital signs such as heart rate, oxygen levels, and blood pressure in real time. Alerts generated by these systems allow medical professionals to intervene rapidly during emergencies, improving patient outcomes.

The rise of edge computing has further enhanced real-time analytics by bringing data processing closer to the source. In scenarios where data must be analyzed with ultra-low latency or where bandwidth is limited, edge devices perform local computations and send only critical results to centralized systems. This architecture is especially valuable in industrial automation, autonomous vehicles, and remote healthcare applications. By reducing the time it takes for data to travel and be processed, edge analytics supports applications that demand immediate reaction and autonomy.

Despite its advantages, implementing real-time data analysis comes with technical and organizational challenges. Ensuring data quality in real time is difficult, as there is limited time for validation or cleaning. Inconsistent or incomplete data can lead to incorrect decisions if not properly handled. Systems must be designed to manage errors gracefully and apply mechanisms such as data buffering, retries, and fallbacks. Scalability is another concern, as systems must handle fluctuations in data volume without degradation in performance. This requires careful capacity planning, load balancing, and the ability to scale horizontally across distributed infrastructure.

Security and compliance are also critical in real-time analytics environments. Sensitive data flowing through real-time pipelines must be encrypted and access-controlled to prevent unauthorized usage. Organizations must comply with data protection regulations that govern the collection and processing of personal information, even in high-speed contexts. Auditing, logging, and traceability must be built into real-time systems to ensure accountability and transparency.

The human element plays a crucial role in the success of real-time data analysis. Analysts, engineers, and decision-makers must be equipped with the skills to design, interpret, and act on real-time insights. Training, process alignment, and cross-functional collaboration are necessary to integrate real-time capabilities into the organizational culture. The shift from traditional batch-oriented thinking to real-time responsiveness requires not only technical changes but also a new mindset that embraces speed, agility, and continuous adaptation.

Real-time data analysis represents a new frontier in how organizations understand and respond to the world. It enables a level of responsiveness that aligns with the fast-paced nature of modern business and society. Whether it is preventing fraud, optimizing supply chains, or delivering real-time content recommendations, the ability to analyze data in the moment is a powerful enabler of innovation, efficiency, and competitive advantage. As technologies evolve and real-time capabilities become more accessible, the demand for systems that can act on data instantly will continue to grow, reshaping how decisions are made and how services are delivered.

Scaling Data Science with Big Data Tools

As data continues to grow in volume, variety, and velocity, traditional data science workflows face limitations in storage, processing speed, and analytical capacity. Datasets that once fit neatly into a spreadsheet now span terabytes or even petabytes, coming from diverse sources like transaction logs, social media, IoT sensors, mobile applications, and streaming platforms. Scaling data science in this context requires not only more powerful hardware but also the adoption of big data tools and architectures designed to process large-scale information efficiently and in a distributed fashion. The integration of big data technologies into data science workflows enables analysts, engineers, and researchers to extract meaningful insights from massive datasets without being constrained by computational bottlenecks.

The core principle of scaling data science is distributing the workload across multiple machines so that tasks can be executed in parallel. This distribution addresses both the storage and processing needs of large datasets. Hadoop was one of the earliest frameworks to popularize distributed storage and computation through its Hadoop Distributed File System and MapReduce paradigm. HDFS enables the storage of large datasets by splitting them into smaller blocks and distributing them across a cluster of nodes. MapReduce allows computation to be performed close to the data, minimizing data transfer and improving efficiency. While Hadoop laid the foundation for big data processing, it was eventually supplanted by more flexible and faster frameworks such as Apache Spark.

Apache Spark revolutionized big data processing by introducing in-memory computing, which dramatically improves the speed of iterative machine learning algorithms and real-time analytics. Spark's ability to process data in memory, combined with its resilient distributed datasets, provides fault tolerance and performance advantages over disk-based systems. Spark's MLlib library includes scalable implementations of common machine learning algorithms, including regression, classification, clustering, and recommendation systems. Data scientists can build, train, and validate models on large datasets using familiar interfaces such as PySpark, which bridges Python's ease of use with Spark's distributed computing power. This enables analysts to experiment and iterate without downsampling their data, preserving accuracy and generalizability.

Data wrangling and transformation at scale are also essential components of big data workflows. Tools like Apache Hive and Apache Pig allow users to write SQL-like queries or scripts that operate over massive datasets stored in Hadoop or similar systems. Apache Flink provides robust support for stream processing, making it ideal for scenarios where real-time insights are needed from continuously flowing data. Dask, an open-source parallel computing library for Python, allows users to scale their data science code by replacing standard data structures like pandas DataFrames or NumPy arrays with distributed counterparts. These tools help automate and parallelize data cleaning, feature engineering, and transformation processes, which are often the most time-consuming parts of data science projects.

Another important aspect of scaling data science is the integration of distributed data storage systems. NoSQL databases such as Apache Cassandra, MongoDB, and HBase are optimized for handling unstructured or semi-structured data at scale. These databases are designed for high availability, horizontal scalability, and fast read-write performance. They enable real-time access to large volumes of data, which is critical for applications such as recommendation systems, fraud detection, and personalization engines. In addition to NoSQL systems, cloud-based storage solutions like Amazon S3, Google Cloud Storage, and Azure Data Lake provide elastic storage capacity and integrate seamlessly with big data processing engines. Cloud storage reduces the infrastructure burden and allows teams to focus on analysis rather than hardware management.

Workflow orchestration is another key consideration when scaling data science with big data tools. Managing the execution of complex pipelines that involve data ingestion, transformation, model training, evaluation, and deployment requires robust orchestration frameworks. Apache Airflow, Luigi, and Prefect are popular tools that allow teams to define workflows as directed acyclic graphs, schedule tasks, monitor execution, and handle failures gracefully. These tools ensure that big data pipelines run reliably and consistently, even as they grow in complexity and scale.

Scaling machine learning also means dealing with the challenges of model training and serving in distributed environments. Frameworks such as TensorFlow and PyTorch now offer support for distributed training, enabling models to be trained across multiple GPUs or nodes. Horovod and Ray provide additional capabilities for scaling deep learning and reinforcement learning workloads. Model serving platforms like TensorFlow Serving, MLflow, and Seldon Core allow trained models to be deployed at scale with high availability and low latency. These platforms integrate with Kubernetes and other container orchestration systems to ensure that model inference can handle production-level traffic and dynamically adjust to changing demands.

Data governance, security, and compliance become increasingly important as data science scales. Ensuring data quality, lineage, and privacy across large, distributed systems requires robust metadata management and auditing tools. Apache Atlas and Amundsen provide metadata management solutions that track dataset usage, ownership, and schema evolution. Role-based access control and encryption mechanisms ensure that data is protected both in transit and at rest. Compliance with regulations such as GDPR and HIPAA must be maintained even when data spans multiple storage systems and processing frameworks. Organizations must implement clear policies and monitoring tools to manage access, usage, and retention of data at scale.

Collaboration and reproducibility are crucial in large-scale data science projects. Version control for code, data, and models is facilitated by tools like Git, DVC, and MLflow. These tools enable teams to track changes, share results, and reproduce experiments in distributed environments. Notebook environments such as JupyterHub and Databricks allow multiple users to collaborate on shared datasets and run computations on distributed backends. Containerization with Docker and orchestration with Kubernetes further support reproducibility by standardizing environments across development, testing, and production stages.

Cloud computing platforms provide the infrastructure backbone for scalable data science. Services like AWS EMR, Azure Synapse, and Google BigQuery offer managed solutions that combine storage, processing, and analytics capabilities. These platforms allow organizations to scale elastically, paying only for the resources they use. Serverless computing models further simplify scaling by abstracting infrastructure management entirely. By using cloud-native tools and services, data science teams can accelerate innovation, reduce operational overhead, and deliver insights faster.

Scaling data science with big data tools is not just about handling more data; it is about unlocking new capabilities that were previously impossible. It allows organizations to analyze entire datasets instead of samples, detect patterns in real time, and personalize experiences at the individual level. It empowers researchers to explore complex phenomena with unprecedented depth and granularity. As data continues to grow, the ability to scale data science workflows using the right tools and architectures will be a defining factor in the success of data-driven organizations. Embracing distributed systems, automation, and collaborative practices ensures that data science can continue to evolve and deliver value in an increasingly data-saturated world.

The Future of Data Science

The future of data science is being shaped by a confluence of technological advances, evolving business demands, and increasing societal expectations. As data continues to grow in scale, complexity, and importance, data science is moving beyond its traditional boundaries and becoming a foundational element of innovation, strategy, and decision-making in virtually every sector. What began as a niche discipline focused on statistical analysis and machine learning has expanded into an interdisciplinary field that intersects with artificial intelligence, cloud computing, ethics, and human-centered design. The trajectory of data science suggests a future where data-driven intelligence is deeply embedded into daily life, transforming industries, institutions, and individual experiences.

One of the defining trends in the future of data science is the growing integration of artificial intelligence. Machine learning models are becoming more autonomous, capable of not only learning from data but also optimizing their own structures and parameters through processes like neural architecture search and meta-learning. These developments reduce the need for manual tuning and enable the creation of more adaptive, generalizable models. The future will see increased use of self-supervised and unsupervised learning techniques, which can extract insights from vast amounts of unlabeled data, expanding the scope of what machines can learn without human input. As AI systems become more capable, data scientists will shift from crafting algorithms by hand to designing ecosystems where intelligent agents can learn, collaborate, and evolve.

Another major force shaping the future of data science is the democratization of tools and platforms. Low-code and no-code environments are making it easier for non-technical users to access and utilize data science capabilities. Automated machine learning systems guide users through the entire modeling process, from data cleaning to model selection and evaluation. These tools lower the barrier to entry and enable domain experts, such as healthcare professionals, educators, and policymakers, to harness data without needing deep technical expertise. This democratization will lead to broader participation in data-driven problem-solving and foster innovation in areas traditionally underserved by advanced analytics.

Edge computing and the Internet of Things are also playing a significant role in the evolution of data science. As more devices become connected and capable of collecting data, the demand for real-time analysis at the edge will increase. This shift requires data scientists to develop models that are lightweight, efficient, and capable of operating under resource constraints. Federated learning and on-device AI are emerging as key technologies that allow data to be analyzed locally, preserving privacy and reducing latency. These methods are especially important in sensitive domains like healthcare and finance, where data cannot be easily transferred to centralized servers. The future of data science includes a growing focus on decentralized intelligence, where models are trained and deployed across distributed networks of devices.

The increasing emphasis on ethics, fairness, and transparency will continue to influence how data science is practiced and perceived. As algorithms become more influential in shaping decisions about employment, credit, healthcare, and criminal justice, there is a growing demand for accountability and explainability. Future data science will involve not just building accurate models but also ensuring that they are interpretable, unbiased, and aligned with human values. Frameworks for responsible AI development will become standard, incorporating fairness audits, impact assessments, and community engagement into the model development lifecycle. Data scientists will be expected to possess a strong ethical foundation and to collaborate with ethicists, legal experts, and social scientists to navigate the broader implications of their work.

In the coming years, the role of the data scientist is also expected to evolve. While technical skills will remain important, the ability to understand context, communicate insights, and influence strategic decisions will become increasingly valuable. Data scientists will work more closely with business leaders, product managers, and UX designers to ensure that analytical solutions are aligned with organizational goals and user needs. The hybrid professional, one who combines technical fluency with domain expertise and communication skills, will become the norm. Education and training programs will adapt by emphasizing interdisciplinary learning, critical thinking, and collaboration.

Quantum computing holds transformative potential for data science, offering the possibility to solve problems that are currently intractable for classical computers. Quantum algorithms may dramatically accelerate tasks such as optimization, simulation, and cryptography, enabling breakthroughs in fields ranging from materials science to logistics. While practical quantum computing remains in its early stages, data scientists are beginning to explore quantum machine learning, quantum data encoding, and hybrid classical-quantum systems. Preparing for this future involves building foundational knowledge of quantum mechanics, linear algebra, and probabilistic reasoning, as well as engaging with emerging quantum development frameworks.

Natural language processing will continue to grow in sophistication and impact, enabling machines to understand, generate, and translate human language with increasing nuance. Large language models are evolving into foundational models that can perform a wide range of tasks with minimal fine-tuning. These models will become integral tools for knowledge discovery, content creation, customer support, and human-computer interaction. As these systems become more conversational and context-aware, data scientists will focus on refining prompt engineering, aligning models with user intent, and mitigating the risks of misinformation or misuse.

The integration of data science into public policy and social impact initiatives is another area of growth. Governments and nonprofits are increasingly using data to inform decision-making, design interventions, and evaluate outcomes. From urban planning and environmental monitoring to public health and education reform, data science is enabling evidence-based approaches to complex societal challenges. As the field matures, data scientists will be called upon to ensure that their analyses are inclusive, representative, and actionable, contributing to more equitable and sustainable outcomes.

Augmented analytics and human-in-the-loop systems will redefine the relationship between humans and machines. Rather than replacing human judgment, data science tools will enhance it by providing context, surfacing insights, and offering decision support. Visualization, storytelling, and interactive dashboards will remain crucial for bridging the gap between data and understanding. In collaborative environments, humans and AI will work together to explore hypotheses, simulate scenarios, and test strategies, leading to more informed and confident decisions.

The future of data science is not limited to technical evolution but also involves cultural and organizational transformation. Companies that embrace a data-driven mindset will cultivate environments where experimentation is encouraged, data is treated as a strategic asset, and insights are embedded into everyday workflows. Leaders will need to champion data literacy across all levels of the organization, ensuring that employees have the skills and tools needed to engage with data meaningfully. As the volume and complexity of data continue to expand, the ability to extract value from it will define competitive advantage.

Data science stands at the intersection of possibility and responsibility. The next generation of data scientists will shape not only the technologies of the future but also the norms and principles that govern their use. With the right mix of curiosity, rigor, and empathy, they will help build systems that are intelligent, transparent, and aligned with the common good. The path ahead is filled with challenges, but also with the opportunity to reimagine how data can enhance human potential and solve some of the world's most pressing problems. The future of data science promises to be as complex as the data it seeks to understand, and as dynamic as the world it aims to improve.

Building a Career in Data Science

Building a career in data science involves more than just learning to manipulate data or train machine learning models. It requires a thoughtful combination of technical proficiency, business acumen, curiosity, communication skills, and the ability to continuously adapt in a rapidly changing field. Data science is inherently interdisciplinary, blending elements of statistics, computer science, mathematics, and domain-specific knowledge to derive actionable insights from data. As industries across the globe embrace digital transformation, the demand for skilled data scientists continues to grow, offering diverse opportunities for professionals who are ready to navigate complex challenges and create value through data.

The journey into data science often begins with acquiring a strong foundation in mathematics and statistics. Understanding concepts such as probability distributions, hypothesis testing, linear algebra, and calculus is essential for designing algorithms, interpreting results, and validating models. These mathematical principles form the backbone of machine learning and data analysis, allowing practitioners to evaluate the reliability and significance of their findings. Alongside this, a solid grasp of statistics enables data scientists to assess variability, identify patterns, and make data-driven decisions in the face of uncertainty. Mastery of these fundamental concepts is not merely academic but crucial for practical application.

Programming skills are equally important in a data science career. Proficiency in languages such as Python or R is necessary for data manipulation, visualization, and model development. Python, in particular, has become the industry standard due to its extensive ecosystem of libraries like NumPy, pandas, Scikit-learn, TensorFlow, and PyTorch. R remains valuable in statistical analysis and academic research. Familiarity with SQL is also critical, as much of the data used in industry resides in relational databases. Understanding how to query, filter, and join data efficiently is essential for preparing datasets for analysis. As data becomes increasingly complex and voluminous, knowledge of big data tools such as Apache Spark and distributed computing platforms also becomes advantageous.

Data scientists must also develop strong data wrangling and preprocessing capabilities. Real-world data is often messy, incomplete, or inconsistent, requiring significant cleaning and transformation before analysis. Knowing how to handle missing values, detect outliers, normalize variables, and engineer features can significantly influence the performance of models. These skills distinguish effective data scientists who can work with raw data from those who rely solely on curated datasets. The ability to understand and manipulate data in its native form is a critical differentiator in the field.

Once the foundational skills are in place, aspiring data scientists should focus on building a portfolio of projects that demonstrate their capabilities. Portfolios allow employers to assess both technical competence and the ability to solve real-world problems. Projects might include analyzing publicly available datasets, developing predictive models, building dashboards, or conducting exploratory data analysis. These projects should be well-documented, clearly communicate objectives and outcomes, and include code that is clean, modular, and reproducible. Publishing work on platforms such as GitHub, Kaggle, or personal blogs helps establish credibility and visibility within the data science community. Participating in competitions or contributing to open-source projects further enhances practical experience and networking opportunities.

Communication is a vital skill in data science careers. The ability to explain technical concepts to non-technical stakeholders, translate complex analyses into actionable insights, and present findings through compelling narratives is crucial for driving impact. Data scientists must be able to tell the story behind the data, connecting analytics to business outcomes and strategic goals. This requires empathy, an understanding of the audience, and the ability to distill complexity without oversimplification. Visualization tools such as Matplotlib, Seaborn, Plotly, and Tableau support this storytelling process, allowing insights to be conveyed through clear and engaging graphics.

Understanding the business context is essential for delivering relevant and impactful solutions. Data scientists who grasp the strategic objectives of their organization can prioritize problems effectively, design models that align with business goals, and measure success in terms that stakeholders understand. This requires collaboration with product managers, marketers, engineers, and executives to define problems, align expectations, and integrate solutions into decision-making processes. The most successful data scientists are those who blend analytical rigor with a deep understanding of the industry and a focus on creating tangible value.

The career path in data science is not linear and can vary depending on interests and expertise. Entry-level roles such as data analyst, junior data scientist, or machine learning engineer provide a foothold in the industry. Over time, professionals may specialize in areas such as natural language processing, computer vision, deep learning, or MLOps. Others may transition into leadership roles, managing teams of data scientists and guiding the strategic use of analytics within an organization. Academic research, consulting, entrepreneurship, and product development are also viable avenues, each offering unique challenges and rewards.

Continuous learning is a defining feature of a successful data science career. The field evolves rapidly, with new techniques, tools, and frameworks emerging constantly. Staying up to date requires a commitment to lifelong learning through online courses, certifications, conferences, journals, and community engagement. Platforms such as Coursera, edX, Udacity, and DataCamp provide access to high-quality content across a wide range of topics. Reading academic papers, participating in meetups, and following thought leaders on social media contribute to staying informed and inspired. Curiosity and a growth mindset are essential traits for thriving in this dynamic environment.

Mentorship and networking play an important role in career development. Learning from experienced professionals can accelerate growth, provide guidance during transitions, and offer insights into industry best practices. Building relationships through professional associations, conferences, and online communities helps open doors to new opportunities and fosters a sense of belonging within the data science ecosystem. Sharing knowledge through teaching, writing, or public speaking further reinforces learning and establishes a personal brand.

A career in data science is both intellectually stimulating and deeply rewarding. It offers the opportunity to tackle complex problems, work at the intersection of technology and business, and contribute to meaningful outcomes in areas such as healthcare, education, finance, and sustainability. For those who are passionate about learning, solving puzzles, and making a difference through data, data science provides a rich and evolving landscape of possibilities. With the right mix of technical skills, communication ability, and business awareness, aspiring data scientists can build impactful careers and become catalysts for innovation and change in the data-driven world.

www.ingramcontent.com/pod-product-compliance
Lightning Source LLC
LaVergne TN
LVHW022318060326
832902LV00020B/3534